DISCOVERING U.S. HISTORY

World War II
1939–1945

Tim McNeese

Consulting Editor: Richard Jensen, Ph.D.

CHELSEA HOUSE
PUBLISHERS
An imprint of Infobase Publishing

WORLD WAR II: 1939–1945

Copyright © 2010 by Infobase Publishing

All rights reserved. No part of this book may be reproduced or utilized in
any form or by any means, electronic or mechanical, including photocopying,
recording, or by any information storage or retrieval systems, without
permission in writing from the publisher. For information contact:

Chelsea House
An imprint of Infobase Publishing
132 West 31st Street
New York NY 10001

Library of Congress Cataloging-in-Publication Data
McNeese, Tim.
  World War II, 1939–1945 / by Tim McNeese.
      p. cm. — (Discovering U.S. History)
  Includes bibliographical references and index.
  ISBN 978-1-60413-358-5 (hardcover : acid-free paper) 1. World War,
1939–1945—Juvenile literature. 2. World War, 1939–1945—United
States—Juvenile literature. I. Title. II. Title: World War Two,
1939–1945. III. Title: World War 2, 1939-1945. IV. Series.

  D743.7.M376 2010
  940.53—dc22

                        2009029511

Chelsea House books are available at special discounts when purchased in
bulk quantities for businesses, associations, institutions, or sales promotions.
Please call our Special Sales Department in New York at (212) 967-8800
or (800) 322-8755.

You can find Chelsea House on the World Wide Web at http://www.chelseahouse.com

The Discovering U.S. History series was produced for Chelsea House by
Bender Richardson White, Uxbridge, UK

Editors: Lionel Bender and Susan Malyan
Designer and Picture Researcher: Ben White
Production: Kim Richardson
Maps and graphics: Stefan Chabluk
Cover design: Alicia Post

Cover printed by Bang Printing, Brainerd, MN
Book printed and bound by Bang Printing, Brainerd, MN
Date printed: April 2010
Printed in the United States of America

10 9 8 7 6 5 4 3 2 1

This book is printed on acid-free paper.

All links and web addresses were checked and verified to be correct at the time of publication. Because of
the dynamic nature of the web, some addresses and links may have changed since publication and may no
longer be valid.

Contents

Introduction: Into the Abyss of War 7

Map: A Military Nation, 1939 to 1945 12

1 Early Signs of War 15

2 American Isolationism 27

3 New Challenges and War 38

4 War Comes to America 51

5 A Two-Front War 64

6 The Home Front 82

7 Victory for the Allies 97

Chronology and Timeline 116

Glossary 123

Bibliography 127

Further Resources 129

Picture Credits 131

Index 132

About the Author and Consultant 136

Introduction
Into the Abyss of War

Before dawn on December 7, 1941, 200 miles (320 kilometers) north of the Hawaiian island of Oahu, nearly 200 Japanese planes were ready to lift off from the decks of six aircraft carriers. The young pilots and crews of the Japanese Strike Force had been awakened at 3:30 that morning. As each man dressed for war, he donned a new loin cloth, called a *mawashi*, and a special "thousand-stitch" belt. According to tradition, each stitch represented a prayer said on behalf of the wearer. Before boarding their planes, the pilots wrapped their *hachimaki* around their heads and over their helmets. *Hachimaki* were traditional white headbands, featuring a red circle that symbolized the Rising Sun of Imperial Japan. Pilots and other personnel gathered around small Shinto shrines for prayers and meditation, aware of the importance of their day's mission. At breakfast the young men ate red rice and fish, a dish usually reserved for times of celebration.

FILLING THE SKIES

Once in their planes, the Japanese pilots revved their engines. The seas were rolling that morning, making takeoff a bit difficult, but the sky was only slightly cloudy. The planes were lined up on the decks of the various carriers: the Zeros, the high-levels, the dive bombers, and the torpedo planes. When the order was given, the planes left the decks of the carriers in rapid order, soared across the waves, and massed together at 13,000 feet (4,000 meters). It took some 15 minutes for all the planes to clear the decks, breaking their record practice time. The crewmen onboard the six launch ships cheered and waved to their comrades as each took off into the early morning sky. Few, if any, of the pilots in the massed squadrons had ever seen so many planes in the air at the same time. For the next hour and a half the largest airborne strike force in history headed south toward its target, the island of Oahu, home to U.S. naval, army, and air force bases.

For most of the 50,000 U.S. servicemen and women stationed in Hawaii, the islands were a paradise far removed from the scene of war. For several years fighting had engulfed dozens of nations from Europe to Asia, yet the United States had remained out of the ever-expanding conflict. Hawaii's beautiful landscape and balmy climate made it difficult for the soldiers and sailors to focus on the possibility of attack.

THE APPROACH OF WAR

Flying his high-level bomber, the Japanese squadron's leader, Commander Mitsuo Fuchida, listened to a weather report broadcast over KGMB, a commercial radio station based in the Hawaiian capital of Honolulu. The station had remained on the air through the early morning hours of December 7 at the request of the U.S. Navy on the basis that it was providing a homing beacon for a dozen U.S. long-range bombers, known as B-17s, due into Hawaii from California. The

B-17s were scheduled to arrive at the moment the Japanese planes planned to begin bombing the military installations on Oahu. The Americans, however, were not aware of the presence of the massive Japanese Strike Force or of its plans. The American radio station announcer forecast clouds over the islands, particularly the mountainous areas. Fuchida was pleased; the clouds would help hide his planes until the moment of attack.

At the same time, in the waters off the coast of Oahu, U.S. naval personnel began having curious encounters with the approaching enemy. One U.S. vessel, a mine sweeper named *Condor,* spotted a submarine periscope in waters closed to U.S. submarines. The men on the *Condor* contacted another ship, the *Ward*, a World War I-era destroyer, and the two vessels began searching for the sub. The gunnery officer onboard the *Ward* went below decks and awakened the ship's young skipper, Lieutenant William Outerbridge. Wearing a Japanese kimono, Lt. Outerbridge came on deck and peered out into the black sky. This was his first patrol, and he did not intend to make a mistake. He ordered all hands on deck to look for the unidentified submarine. Thirty minutes of searching yielded no visual contact. Outerbridge ordered those not on regular watch to return to their bunks.

Outerbridge chose not to report the incident to shore head-quarters, even though the *Ward's* crew continued searching the dark water. By 5 A.M., three additional ships had joined the hunt. At 6:30 searchers aboard yet another ship, the USS *Antares,* spotted the submarine. Three minutes later a navy patrol plane saw the underwater craft and radioed in its location. In less than 10 minutes the *Ward* steamed into the same waters and Outerbridge himself spotted the sub less than 100 yards (90 m) away, headed in the direction of Pearl Harbor. The lieutenant gave the order and deck gunners began firing at the unauthorized submarine.

The blast of shipboard guns tore through the dawn of an otherwise quiet Sunday morning on Oahu. The *Ward's* No. 1 gun missed its target, but the artillery men on the ship's No. 3 gun made a direct hit on the sub's conning tower, or pilot house. At that moment a patrol plane flew in low, dropping several depth charges in the dark waters. Soon the Japanese midget sub bobbed to the surface, slipped onto its side, and began to sink. The *Ward's* radio officer tapped out a coded message dictated by Outerbridge to headquarters:

WE HAVE ATTACKED, FIRED UPON AND DROPPED DEPTH CHARGES UPON SUBMARINE OPERATING IN DEFENSIVE SEA AREA.

Three U.S. battleships are stricken in Pearl Harbor by Japanese fighter planes. They are, left to right, USS *West Virginia* (severely damaged); USS *Tennessee* (damaged); and USS *Arizona* (eventually sank).

The time was now 6:53 A.M. The message of the submarine encounter was delivered to Rear Admiral C. C. Bloch, Commandant of the 14th Naval District. After conferring with the fleet duty officer, Captain John B. Earle, Bloch decided that the report was nothing to worry about. For the moment, he chose to take no action.

TORA! TORA! TORA!

The three hours that passed between the spotting of the Japanese submarine and the first bombs falling on Pearl Harbor are the most critical hours in U.S. history. By 7:55 A.M., Commander Fuchida's formation of Japanese attack planes had reached their unsuspecting targets, docked in Pearl Harbor. Fuchida broke radio silence at 7:49 A.M., gleeful that his planes had gone undetected until the final minutes before the attack. Radioing his fellow pilots, Fuchida said: *"To-To-To,"* the first syllable of the Japanese word for "charge." Then, almost immediately, the Japanese commander repeated: *"Tora! Tora! Tora!"* *Tora*, the Japanese word for "tiger," was the designated term to indicate that the Americans below were not prepared. To tell the pilots flying planes without radios of the good news, Fuchida fired a blue flare into the early morning sky. The Japanese surprise attack against U.S. naval forces on the Hawaiian island of Oahu was underway.

In another two hours, it would all be over. This attack would become the single worst military disaster in the history of the U.S. Navy and would bring the United States into the most destructive war in the history of humankind. Why did the Japanese military unleash a full-scale attack against U.S. installations on that fateful day in early December? What had brought these two nations from a relationship of peace to that of enemies? How had the United States, whose citizens were so fearful of war and so determined to remain at peace, immediately fallen into the abyss of war?

A Military Nation, 1939 to 1945

Although there was no fighting on the U.S. mainland during World War II, parts of the country were designated as military areas. This led to setting up relocation or internment camps to house people of Japanese ancestry throughout the war. Other camps were set up to house German and Italian prisoners of war.

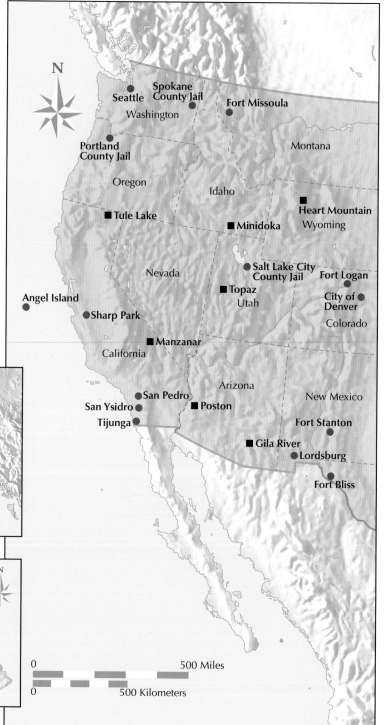

Seattle
Spokane County Jail
Fort Missoula
Washington
Portland County Jail
Oregon
Idaho
Montana
Tule Lake
Minidoka
Heart Mountain
Wyoming
Salt Lake City County Jail
Fort Logan
Nevada
Topaz
Utah
City of Denver
Colorado
Angel Island
Sharp Park
Manzanar
California
Arizona
New Mexico
San Pedro
San Ysidro
Poston
Tijunga
Fort Stanton
Gila River
Lordsburg
Fort Bliss

ALASKA

N

0   500 Miles
0   500 Kilometers

Camp Honouliuli
Sand Island
HAWAIIAN ISLANDS

N

0   150 Miles
0   150 Kilometers

0   500 Miles
0   500 Kilometers

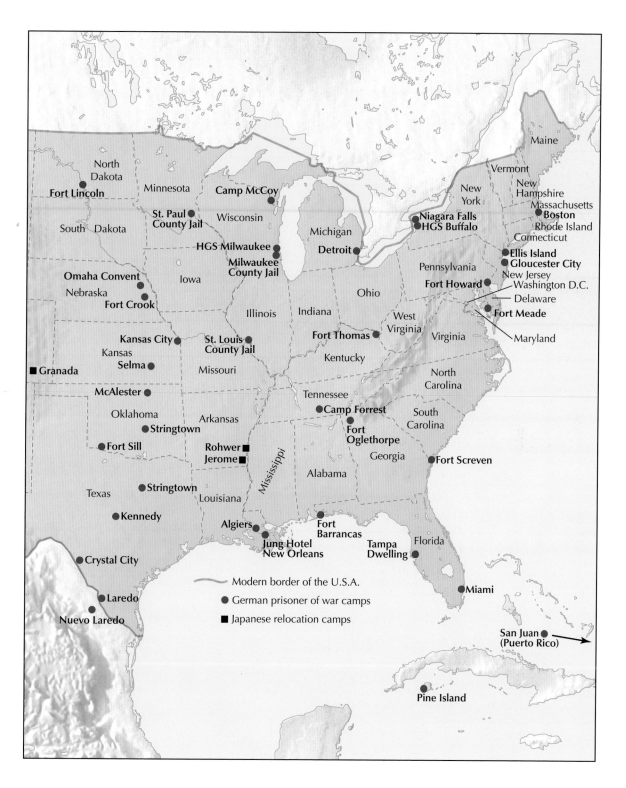

North Dakota

Fort Lincoln

Minnesota

Camp McCoy

Maine

Vermont

New Hampshire

St. Paul County Jail

Wisconsin

New York

Massachusetts

Boston

South Dakota

Rhode Island

Connecticut

Michigan

Niagara Falls HGS Buffalo

HGS Milwaukee

Milwaukee County Jail

Detroit

Pennsylvania

Ellis Island

Gloucester City

New Jersey

Washington D.C.

Delaware

Omaha Convent

Iowa

Ohio

Fort Howard

Nebraska

Fort Crook

Illinois

Indiana

West Virginia

Fort Meade

Maryland

Kansas City

St. Louis County Jail

Kentucky

Virginia

Kansas

Selma

Missouri

North Carolina

■ **Granada**

Fort Thomas

McAlester

Tennessee

Camp Forrest

South Carolina

Oklahoma

Arkansas

Stringtown

Fort Oglethorpe

Georgia

Fort Sill

Rohwer ■

Jerome ■

Fort Screven

Alabama

Texas

Stringtown

Louisiana

Mississippi

Kennedy

Algiers

Fort Barrancas

Jung Hotel New Orleans

Tampa Dwelling

Florida

Crystal City

Miami

⌒ Modern border of the U.S.A.

● German prisoner of war camps

■ Japanese relocation camps

Laredo

Nuevo Laredo

San Juan (Puerto Rico) ●→

Pine Island

1
Early Signs of War

In 1933, as the newly elected Democratic President, Franklin Delano Roosevelt, prepared to take office, much of the Western world was in chaos and upheaval. Two threats loomed large—the worldwide economic depression and the rise of dictators from Asia to Europe. Yet even as these larger-than-life challenges appeared to threaten hundreds of millions of people around the world, most U.S. citizens were not prepared to support their government in taking on any immediate role of responsibility other than in its own backyard. FDR felt much the same way. He had a fight of his own, and that was to battle the Great Depression, an economic stagnation that had battered the United States since the stock market crash in October 1929.

A CHANGING PERSPECTIVE

Immediately upon taking the oath of office on March 4, the president began hammering out a recovery agenda he called his New Deal, which included nationwide programs to create work, banking reform and stabilization, extensive changes in monetary policy, and a host of other hopeful remedies. One example of Roosevelt's single-minded agenda to battle the Depression in the United States was his response to the London Economic Conference, an international meeting of representatives of 66 nations held in the summer of 1933.

BEYOND AMERICA'S ISOLATION

As dictators rose to power in Europe and Asia during the early 1930s, President Roosevelt counted himself among the majority of Americans who did not want to see the United States become embroiled in another war or other costly international venture. This policy did not, however, keep FDR from engaging in some forms of international cooperation or foreign policy outreach.

He did, after all, take overt steps to alter the relationship (or lack of one) with the Soviet Union. Since 1917, when the Russians had overthrown Czar Nicholas II and brought a revolutionary Communist government to power, the United States had refused to carry on diplomatic relations with the new Soviet state. But, early in his first term, Roosevelt formally recognized

the Soviet Union. The move led to a storm of protest from conservatives, as well as Roman Catholics and other religious groups who did not like the Soviet practice of stifling religion. Guiding Roosevelt's move to break 16 years of ignoring the Soviet Union were the realities of the Depression. The president thought the United States might become a major trade partner with the U.S.S.R. In addition, FDR was looking for a European power to counter the challenges represented by the increasingly menacing Germany and Japan.

Back in the Western Hemisphere, Roosevelt also tried to reach out to Latin American countries. Stating in his inaugural address, "I would dedicate this nation to the policy of the Good Neighbor," the president wanted to deepen relationships with

The conference called for dozens of industrialized countries around the world to come together to work out a coordinated plan with which all involved could meet the economic challenges of the day. At first Roosevelt agreed to send his secretary of state, Cordell Hull, to the conference. But when the delegates began discussing such issues as stabilizing nations' currencies, FDR, while traveling on Navy cruiser

nations in South and Central America. This move meant FDR was interested in the United States playing a major regional role as a world power, rather than a leading role in Europe or Asia.

Roosevelt took serious steps to achieve this end. In his first year in office he sent U.S. delegates to the Seventh Pan-American Conference in Uruguay, where they voted on a resolution supporting nonintervention in the Western Hemisphere. The United States had been guilty of intervention many times over during the previous two generations. In 1934, FDR pulled the last U.S. Marines out of Haiti, where they had been for decades. Similarly, the United States declared it had no intentions of interfering in Cuba, even after a military coup in 1934. Two years later the United States relaxed its use of power in the Canal Zone in Panama.

The true test of FDR's "Good Neighbor" policy came in 1938, when the Mexican government took control of U.S. oil interests on Mexican soil. Although U.S. company officials begged Roosevelt to intervene, he refused, instead helping to settle the dispute by 1941, even as U.S. companies lost millions in former investments in Mexico. Ultimately, such moves were seen as friendly gestures toward Latin America by the very nations they were meant to impress. (Providing even greater good will was the Reciprocal Trade Agreements Act that Roosevelt pushed through Congress, which lowered tariff rates in trade with countries, including Latin America.) When FDR visited the Inter-American Conference for the Maintenance of Peace in Argentina in 1936, he was received by cheering crowds as a friend and hero.

USS *Indianapolis*, sent a radio message to London that he was pulling the U.S. delegation out. He was so concerned that his economic recovery plan would be undermined that he withdrew, causing the London Conference to fall apart within only a few days of starting.

During his first term in office, however, Roosevelt began to change his views. As events unfolded in Europe, Asia, and elsewhere, the president became convinced that the United States would have to take on a key role in world events. Dictators were coming to power around the world, and they were an aggressive collection of Fascists, Communists, and other political extremists. While many Americans continued to believe that the United States was safe, protected by two great oceans from would-be harm or invasion, FDR saw a larger picture: The nations of the modern world were dependent on one another; no nation was ultimately safe; and the future could not remain in the hands of those ready to enslave or destroy.

A GALLERY OF EVIL

Those men who would challenge the security of the western nations and even the foundations of western civilization itself were a varied group, each with his own extremist philosophy and an agenda to extend power over others. Military leaders came to power in Japan, Italy, and Germany, as they encouraged a build up of their armies and weapons arsenals. Aggression seemed to have become the order of the day.

Some of these dictators were already in power when Roosevelt assumed the presidency in 1933. The ruthless Josef Stalin ruled the Soviet Union as a dictator. With Marxism as his credo, Stalin believed in the ultimate collapse of western capitalism and a final revolution led by the workers of the world. Meanwhile, in Italy, Benito Mussolini and his Fascist party were dedicated to boldfaced expansionism.

GERMANY: ADOLF HITLER

In January 1933, just five weeks before FDR was inaugurated as president, a new leader came to power in Germany's Weimar Republic. Germany had been defeated during World War I, and then crushed by the allied leaders during the peace conference at Versailles in 1919. Its military had been reduced to near zero, with an army of only 100,000, the navy destroyed, and no air force. France and Britain had placed war damages on Germany to the tune of billions of gold marks, which the defeated Germans could not begin to pay in earnest. Many Germans had been humiliated by the way their country had been treated through the Versailles Treaty, and one of those who dedicated themselves to bringing about their nation's recovery was a toothbrush-mustached Fascist named Adolf Hitler.

When the Versailles Treaty reduced Germany to near pauper status at the close of World War I, Austrian-born Hitler was angered and filled with hatred toward those he blamed for Germany's losses, especially Great Britain, France, and the other western democracies that had prostrated his nation at Versailles. Throughout the 1920s he organized a political group opposed to the Weimar Government, the National Socialist German Workers Party, which became known as the Nazis.

Given the unstable economic times, Hitler's task of promoting the rabid racism and right-wing extremism and propaganda of the Nazis was an easy one. During the early 1920s, the German Republic struggled with the effects of a downward-spiraling postwar economy. Unemployment was rampant, and hyperinflation ate up a worker's wages. By 1924, though, through the Dawes Plan, Germany was able to stagger its reparations payments and soon its economy regained traction. For four or five years, Germans enjoyed a bustling prosperity. But these good times rested on foreign loans, mostly from American banks. After the Depression hit Germany hard in 1929, the nation's economy sank once again, leaving open the way for such radical groups as the National Socialists to gain political power.

Hitler Becomes Chancellor

As Hitler became more popular during the late 1920s and early 1930s, he was able to gain political influence. By 1930 his Nazi Party was the most significant minority political group in Germany. When the Great Depression caused the collapse of the German economy in 1930, Hitler was on the scene, offering answers and pointing the finger of blame at Jewish bankers, American capitalists, and Russian Communists.

By 1932 Hitler's National Socialists had 800,000 members and had become the most powerful political organization in Germany. The elections held that summer resulted in the Nazi Party gaining a majority of seats in the German legislature. Hitler, holding the majority support, was able to have himself selected by the aging German president, Paul von Hindenburg, as Germany's chancellor, a role similar to that of a prime minister. By January 30, 1933, Adolf Hitler was the number-two man in all of Germany.

In short order, the doddering Hindenburg was pushed aside, giving Hitler control of the government. He soon began creating a totalitarian state, dismantling the German republican government and replacing officials with his fellow National Socialists. In protest, on the night of February 27, 1933, a Dutch left-wing radical, Marinus van der Lubbe, burned the Reichstag building, the legislative seat of government. Blaming Communists for the fire, Hitler made emergency decrees to take full control of the government, even as he suppressed freedom of speech, assembly, and the press. The last parliamentary election was held that spring, with the Nazis receiving 44 percent of the votes, far more than for any other party. It would be 12 years before such elections were again allowed.

The Third Reich

Then the old president died in August 1934. At that point the office of Reich president was abolished, making Hitler the undisputed leader. He immediately began pursuing a course of rebuilding the dignity and pride of Germany by bringing its military back to life, despite the prohibitions placed on the country by the Treaty of Versailles. As he developed his nation's military capabilities, Hitler drew the attention of the Allied victors of World War I, but weak protests from France and Great Britain meant nothing to him.

The German dictator, known as *der Führer* (the leader), was as methodical as he was cunning. He wasted no time in withdrawing Germany from the League of Nations and, in violation of the Versailles Treaty, rearming. Having huge popular appeal with the German people, Hitler also spoke of the superiority of the Aryan (German) race and of the need to expand the borders of his state, the Third German Empire, or Third Reich, to provide additional territory— *Lebensraum,* or "living space"—for this master race. Equally, Hitler preached a rabid hatred of the Jewish people, whom he considered inferior, even non-human. Before his stranglehold on Germany ended in 1945, Hitler would carry out a racist campaign of extermination against the Jews along with others he considered undesirable.

In the period between his rise to power as chancellor in 1933 and the opening days of World War II in 1939, Hitler increased his power base. He ignored the Versailles Treaty and in 1936 ordered his armies into the German Rhineland, the western lands of his country, bordering France. As Hitler calculated his next steps, he was certain that Great Britain and France would not take bold measures to stop him.

German chancellor Adolf Hitler arriving at the Nazi Party congress in Nuremberg, September 1936. In the center of the third row is Hitler's deputy, Rudolf Hess, who tried to make peace with Britain in 1941.

JAPAN: A MISSION FOR NEW GLORY

In the early 1930s such European nations as Italy and Germany were considered "have-not" nations. Italy had never fully industrialized, and was still a relatively provincial country. Germany, a generation earlier, had been the industrial superpower of Europe, but had been stripped by the victorious Allies of much of its industrial base, as well as many of its natural resources, including coal and iron mines. The Versailles Treaty had not been generous to Italy or Germany. Similarly, the Asian Pacific nation of Japan, which had also fought in World War I, emerged from the war as a "have-not" power, an island country crowded with millions of citizens and lacking natural resources.

More Space, More Raw Materials

Throughout the 1920s and 1930s Japan struggled to adjust to the new world that emerged following World War I. While its economy was still primarily agricultural, rapid population growth, from 56 million in 1920 to 73 million in 1940, had diminished the amount of land suitable for farming. In a nation about the size of California, only one of every six acres was farmland. This put great pressure on the Japanese government to find more space and land for its people. There was an effort to turn away from an economy dependent on agriculture and to develop an industrial base. But the international system of trade barriers and tariffs, established by the United States and other industrial powers, hampered such growth.

Industrial development was also delayed by a shortage of raw materials. Many of the natural resources needed for manufacturing—oil, rubber, tin, iron—were not found in Japan. Some of her Pacific and Asian neighbors did have these materials in abundance, but these nations were typically controlled by European powers. A great colonial movement over the previous half-century had brought dozens of Asian nations under the control of the Dutch, French, and British. East Indian oil went to the Dutch; Southeast Asian rubber found its way to France; and Burmese tin and bauxite (used in the production of aluminum products) sailed off to Great Britain.

Why should Japan, an Asian nation, have to compete to purchase these locally sourced raw materials? Japanese leaders could only wonder and brood. As the greatest nation in Asia, they thought, surely Japan should control Asian markets and trade in its raw materials. When the Depression began during the 1930s, it began to seem that Japan had everything to gain and little to lose if it "freed" its fellow Pacific and Asian nations from European dominance. Such a policy would also give the Japanese more land to settle. The new rallying cry heard across Japan was simple and clear: "Asia for Asians!"

The Rise of the Army

Leading the drive to create an Asian world dominated and controlled by the Japanese were the young men of the Imperial Army. These officers set out early in the 1930s on a mission to bring new glory to their nation. Strongly anti-western in their beliefs, they were also determined to restore honor and prestige to their government.

In the early 1930s the Japanese launched a campaign of recovery and expansion. In 1934 Japan dropped out of a 12-year-old agreement, the Washington Naval Treaty, under which it and other industrialized nations had agreed to limit the size of their navies. The following year Japan shot down any possibility of a new naval treaty during a conference in London. Soon the Asian nation was investing heavily in a massive shipbuilding program that included submarines, battleships, and aircraft carriers.

In 1935 Japan, too, dropped out of the League of Nations. In reality, Japan was interested in expanding its influence and control throughout the continent to bring about "Asia for Japan." Expansionist Japanese "warlords" hungrily eyed China, especially the northern region of resource-rich Manchuria. They also began making plans to seize eventual control of Southeast Asia and the Dutch East Indies.

UNWILLING FOR WAR

Even as these political extremists came to power in Japan, Italy, and Germany, not to mention the rise of the cold-steeled Stalin in the Soviet Union, the vast majority of Americans remained detached, almost unaware of the international situation. Americans had fought in the Great War—a conflict that many in the United States came to call "the European War"—but they had done so with great reluctance. For many years, America had remained extremely isolationist, refusing to be pulled into wars halfway around the world.

The Great War had unfolded for two and one-half years before President Woodrow Wilson had finally risen up and called for direct U.S. involvement. In his view, the very foundations of western civilization were at stake by that fateful spring of 1917. Entering the war so late, American doughboys had engaged in limited fighting, which included only two major battles under U.S. commanders. As soon as the war was won, many Americans were ready for their soldiers to leave Europe and disentangle politically from the war's aftermath.

When Wilson negotiated at Versailles for the creation of his League of Nations, he was met with a resounding "no" from the U.S. Senate and from the American people. There were additional rejections, as well. The United States would not be a part of the French security treaty; it would not forgive Britain's and France's war debts to the U.S. Treasury; it would not even open up European immigration quotas—in fact Congress passed additional restrictive immigration laws in 1921 and 1924. In the years following the Great War, many Americans became uncertain about whether the United States should have participated in the conflict at all. Isolation was the call across the United States.

President Roosevelt seemed a part of these ranks during the early years of his presidency. While he had supported U.S. membership of the League of Nations prior to his election, he abandoned his position once elected. He torpedoed the London Economic Conference to pursue his own monetary policies, leaving Europe swinging in the wind. The president even took immediate steps during his early months in office to reduce the size of the U.S. Army, which at the time included only 140,000 men. Historian David Kennedy notes that Army Chief of Staff Douglas MacArthur protested the cuts during a meeting with Roosevelt, stating angrily that he wanted Roosevelt's name, not his, to be remembered "when we lost the next war, and an American boy, lying in the mud with an enemy bayonet through his belly and an enemy foot on his dying throat, spat out his last curse."

As Franklin Roosevelt came to the presidency in the spring of 1933, clouds were gathering on several international horizons, signaling great conflicts on multiple continents. But all the signs indicated that, bar some unforeseen circumstances, the United States was prepared to sit back and watch a war unfold without any intention of lifting a finger. As for FDR, he seemed ready for his nation to remain at peace at all costs.

2
American Isolationism

Despite the growing threat to world peace by the mid-1930s, the United States remained staunchly opposed to any involvement in a future war. The U.S. peace movement had gained considerable traction during the 1920s and had increased in strength and support into the early 1930s. The movement, led by women, clergy, and college students, claimed 12 million members, and reached an audience of 50 million. Regardless of world events during Roosevelt's first term, the likelihood of the United States being pulled into a war in Europe or Asia seemed so remote it was unthinkable.

THE MARCH OF AGGRESSION

Yet dictators flexed their muscles and sent their armies marching. In 1934 and 1935, Japan was expanding its navy despite earlier agreements, such as the Five-Power Naval Treaty, which the Japanese had signed. In 1935 the Italian

Fascist leader, Benito Mussolini, invaded the African nation of Ethiopia. It was a campaign of reconquest, technically, as Italy had held Ethiopia as a colony during the nineteenth century, only to have been ousted during the 1890s by the Ethiopians. Mussolini's tanks and planes easily subdued their enemies, who brandished spears and out-of-date firearms. Meanwhile, the League of Nations did little, even though its members could have issued economic sanctions, including a cutoff of oil to Italy, which would have rendered Mussolini's military immobile. In 1936 German troops advanced into the Rhineland, which had been demilitarized under the Treaty of Versailles. This overt step, also, could have been met with force by the former Allies. France alone had the power to stop the Germans in their tracks, as Hitler's military was not yet as strong as it would be in a few more years. But no such steps were taken.

The Spanish Civil War

The year 1936 brought additional aggression, this time in Spain, where civil war broke out following an uprising of Spanish troops in Morocco against the democratically elected Spanish Republic. Their leader was a self-proclaimed Fascist, General Francisco Franco, who soon found friends in Hitler and Mussolini. The ruthless Franco promised economic prosperity and political stability to the Spanish people. Over the next three years, Franco and his fellow Fascists fought the Nationalist armies of Spain. Hitler assisted him by supplying weapons of war, including tanks and some of the newest planes emerging from German airplane factories. Before the Spanish Civil War came to an end in 1939, more than 20,000 uniformed Germans would see duty in Spain.

For some, the Spanish Civil War served as a dress rehearsal for World War II. As Hitler and Mussolini supported their fellow Fascist, so the Soviet Union supported the left-leaning

Loyalists, fighting for the government. From America, 3,000 young men and women—mostly Communists—formed the Abraham Lincoln Brigade and went to Spain to fight as volunteers on behalf of the Loyalists.

As for the U.S. government's position, Washington maintained its diplomatic ties with the Loyalist government. Yet Congress, with FDR's agreement, altered the neutrality acts and cut off arms shipments to both the Loyalists and the Fascists. Franco was delighted, notes historian Dominic Tierney, stating: "Roosevelt behaved in the manner of a true gentleman." The United States, it seems, was prepared to pursue peace at any price.

As Mussolini and Hitler combined their support for Franco, so they did with one another. In the fall of 1936 Italy and Germany signed a military alliance and began calling themselves the Axis Powers. The name came from the analogy of having joined their two capitals, Rome and Berlin, by a line, or axis, that cut across Europe, and around which the world would turn in the future. The Rome–Berlin Axis was a clear sign that Fascism was on the march in Europe.

The following year, Japan succeeded in its dominance of China. In 1931 it had invaded the region of Manchuria. On July 7, 1937, Japanese and Chinese troops fought one another at the Marco Polo Bridge near Peking (today's Beijing), ushering in full-scale war between the two Asian powers. Japan soon seized most of the coast and major cities of the main part of China. Some historians consider this turn of events, which included an all-out invasion by the Japanese, as the opening act of World War II.

UNWILLING TO TAKE STEPS

In the meantime, back in the United States, President Roosevelt refused to take any strong stand in opposition to these blatant acts of worldwide aggression. At the time he had few options. In August 1935, FDR had signed off on the first of a series of neutrality acts, passed by Congress in direct response to the Italian invasion of Ethiopia. His cooperation was crucial, since the acts were written with the stipulation that they would only go into effect "when the president determines" that a state of war exists between nations.

Further neutrality acts were passed in 1936 and 1937. These were made in an effort to eliminate some of the factors that had drawn America into World War I, making U.S. involvement in another such conflict difficult. For example, U.S. companies were forbidden to sell arms and munitions to any "belligerent" power or any other nation at war, unless the purchases were made as "cash-and-carry." Such weapons sales had been carried out routinely during World War I, creating an investment on the part of the U.S. government in support of the Allies. Congress's message: Not this time.

Also, under these acts any American choosing to travel on a passenger liner or other ship owned by a belligerent power did so at his or her own risk. This position was a complete turn away from a right considered fundamental by the United States since its founding—freedom of the seas. Again, the German sinking of liners carrying U.S. citizens had helped pull the United States into the Great War, and Congress was now taking steps to avoid a repeat of history. Another restriction made it illegal for Americans to loan money to any belligerent power, as had happened during World War I.

Some historians have suggested that these neutrality acts may have actually encouraged aggression, since the United States was making it clear through the acts that it was not going to do anything that might lead to war, including arming the victims of aggressive dictators. Also, the United States was surrendering any significant international role it might have been able to play in facing down the aggressors.

The Neutrality Acts Are Tested

Yet, with each additional act of aggression, FDR began to alter his position. For a while, he seemed to side with the isolationists, then at other times he appeared ready to ally himself with the internationalists—those who supported a more aggressive U.S. foreign policy in support of the victims of aggression. But, in the fall of 1937, there was a glimmer of hope for those who believed the United States needed to take stronger stances against extremist aggression. Following the Japanese invasion into China in July, FDR responded cleverly by not imposing the neutrality acts, claiming Japan and China had not yet declared war on one another. This allowed him to continue to support China by sending arms. At the same time, Japan could also buy such raw materials as oil, aviation fuel, and scrap iron (none of which were explicitly military in nature), since it was able to pay for its purchases through the "cash-and-carry" provision.

As the fighting continued between the Chinese and Japanese, those sympathetic to China criticized the U.S. government for allowing war-related sales of scrap iron and fuel between the United States and Japan. Newspapers trumpeted headlines that accused the Roosevelt administration of aiding the Japanese war effort. *The Washington Post* issue for August 29 read:

AMERICAN SCRAP IRON PLAYS GRIM ROLE IN FAR EASTERN WAR JAPANESE RAIN DEATH WITH ONE-TIME JUNK

GUNS, BOMBS, AND BATTLESHIPS, ALL MADE FROM OLD METAL, SHIPPED ACROSS THE PACIFIC IN GROWING AMOUNTS

America's neutrality acts were creating, for some nations who were under attack from totalitarian dictators, many more problems than they were preventing. Yet, notes historian David Kennedy, the Roosevelt administration felt it had to walk a thin line between helping the Chinese and not antagonizing, as FDR's secretary of state, Cordell Hull, called them, "the wild, runaway, half-insane men" running Japan.

A scene of destruction outside a hotel in Shanghai following a Japanese air raid in September 1937. The Sino-Japanese war of 1937–1945 resulted in the deaths of 20 million Chinese and 2 million Japanese.

The Quarantine Speech

Japan's invasion of China seems to have altered Roosevelt's mindset concerning the world's aggressors. On October 5, he gave a speech in Chicago in which he used some harsh words for the likes of Hitler, Mussolini, and the Japanese warlords. He had come to believe that, as much as it could with caution, the United States needed to take a more positive stand against worldwide aggression. Now known as the "Quarantine Speech," Roosevelt was launching a trial balloon to see if the American people were ready for greater action on the part of the administration, even if it might push the United States into war. From his speech:

If we are to have a world in which we can breathe freely and live in amity without fear—the peace-loving nations must make a concerted effort to uphold laws and principles on which alone peace can rest secure. When an epidemic of physical disease starts to spread, the community approves and joins in a quarantine of the patients in order to protect the health of the community against the spread of the disease... War is a contagion, whether it be declared or undeclared. There is no escape through mere isolation or neutrality... There must be positive endeavors to preserve peace.

Roosevelt's trial balloon was immediately shot down by isolationists across America. He had stepped out ahead of the mindset of many Americans, who still did not want the United States to make overt moves that might lead to war. The previous spring, a Gallup poll had asked Americans whether they supported efforts to prevent war, or efforts to keep out of any war. Of those polled, 94 percent favored staying out of war.

As 1938 dawned the aggressors continued to advance, with even greater ruthlessness. Japanese forces were attacking along the Chinese coast, striking cities, including Nanking (the Japanese assault there actually began in mid-December of 1937). For weeks Japanese forces ravaged the

MEANWHILE, THE NEW YORK WORLD'S FAIR

As the threat of war spread throughout Asia and Europe, some Americans were preparing for a diversion. Several years earlier, New York City officials had decided to meet the challenges of the Depression by opening a World's Fair, which would provide both jobs and money from the millions of visitors to one of the largest such fairs in history. In the spring of 1939 the New York City World's Fair opened its doors.

It was an unparalleled spectacle. City officials had raised $150 million to organize the fair and develop the 1,200-acre (485-hectare) grounds in Flushing Meadow, Queens—a site that had served previously as a city dump. Much of the grounds had been paved over, but 10,000 trees had been planted, along with 1 million tulips imported directly from Holland. Visitors to the fair reveled in the 300 large-scale buildings that dotted the landscape, housing exhibitions. There were 1,500 exhibitors, from 33 states, 58 countries, and 1,300 businesses—everyone from Ford to Firestone, General Motors to General Electric, and Chrysler to Coca-Cola.

The fair's president, New Yorker Grover Whalen, had named the fair "The World of Tomorrow." It featured the wonders of the most advanced technologies, while saluting the practical values of democracy. Towering over this ambitious international event, at the Fair's Theme Center, was a 700-foot (213-m) tall, needle-shaped pyramid, called a Trylon. Next to it stood a 200-foot (61-m) globe called, well, not a globe, but a "Perisphere." This was, after all, a fair designed not to look back at humankind's past accomplishments, but to provide fairgoers with a peek at the future. Whalen and his fellow planners had created a fair based on streamlined, futuristic architecture, fountains, and razzmatazz (there were music shows and an amusement park at the fair).

city, engaging in barbarous acts of rape, beheading, and disemboweling, and slaughtering innocent Chinese civilians by the thousands. The "Rape of Nanking" rankled Ameri-

So certain of the future were the fair designers that they buried, through the courtesy of the Westinghouse Corporation, a time capsule on the premises, filled with the stuff of daily life: an alarm clock, a set of alphabet blocks, a Mickey Mouse plastic cup, comic strips of Dick Tracy and Little Orphan Annie, a film of Albert Einstein, copies of *Gone With the Wind* and Upton Sinclair's *Arrowsmith*, a piece of asbestos, and the Lord's Prayer in 300 languages. It was all there, placed in a long, sleek, metal cylinder, lowered into a special well, and sealed with a large monkey wrench. The time capsule was intended to be reopened in the future—the distant prospect of 5,000 years later, which would be the year 6939. If the Westinghouse Corporation was nothing in 1939, it was hopeful of the world's future.

The fair seemed stuck on the future. The most popular pavilion at the fair was General Motors' "Futurama." Inside, each visitor—28,000 of them daily—was seated in a special chair on a conveyor belt. This carried its occupant on a 15-minute tour, overlooking an animated scale model, nearly an acre (0.4 ha) large, of what life would be like in America in 1960. The ride's soothing voice-over promised a bright tomorrow: "America in 1960 is full of a tanned and vigorous people who in 20 years have learned how to have fun… Cures for cancer and infantile paralysis have extended man's life span and his wife's skin is still perfect at the age of 75." All those eager visitors, those who stood in the long, switch-back lines to get a glimpse of GM's version of the world of tomorrow, emerged with a button pinned to their shirts and blouses, which simply read: "I have seen the future."

Yet, even as the fair predicted a bright future, the immediate future was clouded with aggression and war. Within six months of the fair's opening, Germany invaded Poland, bringing Britain and France into an ever-expanding world conflict.

cans (another Gallup poll indicated that 59 percent of the Americans asked were sympathetic to the Chinese and only 1 percent favored the Japanese), but few wanted their government to take overt steps.

MORE GERMAN AGGRESSION

Meanwhile, in Europe, Hitler and Mussolini continued their support of General Franco in his civil war against the Loyalists. German planes bombed anti-Fascist strongholds on Spanish soil, allowing pilots to test run the German technologies that were creating a new type of fighting force, one capable of mobilizing quickly for what the Germans were calling *Blitzkrieg,* or lightning war. That spring Hitler took another bold step, as his powerful army moved into Austria on March 11. Within two days he announced the union of Austria and Germany, in the nearly bloodless *Anschluss,* or annexation of Austria.

As Hitler moved toward the east, his next target was Czechoslovakia, a nation that had only existed for 20 years. Cobbled together by the Allies during the Versailles Peace Conference, Czechoslovakia had been formed out of territory formerly controlled by the Austro-Hungarian Empire, to be a nation state homeland for the Czech and Slovak peoples. Ringing the western portion of this state like a horseshoe was the Sudetenland, home to 3 million Germans, many of whom were not happy to be part of Czechoslovakia. Neither was Hitler. Claiming he only wanted "Germany for Germans," the German leader insisted the Czechoslovakian leaders should turn over the Sudetenland to him. They refused.

Tensions began to mount towards the breaking point until, in September 1938, Hitler and Mussolini met with the prime ministers of Great Britain (Neville Chamberlain) and France (Premier Édouard Daladier) in Munich. At the end of the month the leaders of the four countries (the Czechs were not present) came to an agreement known as the Munich Accords: Germany would be granted the Sudetenland. The former Allies were so concerned about keeping the European continent at peace, that they willingly appeased Hitler. (Appeasement is the making of concessions with the hope of satisfying someone else.) Hitler swore that the Sudetenland was all that he had ever wanted, promising, notes historian David Kennedy, that the region was "the last territorial claim I have to make in Europe."

When Prime Minister Chamberlain returned to England, his plane landed at Heathrow Airport, where he emerged and stood on the tarmac waving the agreement in his hand. Before the newsreel cameras, he made a naïve claim: "I believe this to represent peace in our time." Many British subjects cheered Chamberlain's efforts. As for Roosevelt, he sent Chamberlain a congratulatory, two-word cable: "Good Man." Meanwhile, in Parliament, Winston Churchill disagreed, notes historian Alan Axelrod: "England has been offered a choice between war and shame. She has chosen shame and will get war."

Churchill's prediction came true sooner than nearly anyone expected. On March 15, 1939, Hitler's armies smashed across the border in a full-scale invasion of Czechoslovakia. Only six months had passed since the appeasement of the German leader and an agreement that had failed to keep the peace. Within weeks Czechoslovakia was gone, erased by further aggression.

3

New Challenges and War

The western democracies, including Great Britain and France, were shocked when Hitler violated the Munich Accords and sent his armies in to occupy the remainder of Czechoslovakia on March 16, 1939. The British Prime Minister, Neville Chamberlain, vowed to guarantee the sovereignty of Hitler's next likely target in eastern Europe—Poland. Britain and its Commonwealth nations—including Canada, South Africa, India, Australia, and New Zealand—as well as France, were now bound by treaty to aid Poland in case of war.

An invasion of Poland by the Germans would probably mean those western democracies would find themselves working with an unlikely ally—the Soviet Union. While Soviet Communist leader Josef Stalin was no friend of democracy, his political ideology placed him at the opposite end of the political spectrum from Hitler and his Fascists. Stalin would object to a German occupation of Poland, which shared borders with the Soviets. Everything hinged on what Hitler might decide to do next.

The German leader was keenly aware of the challenge the Soviet Union might present to him if he invaded Poland. To neutralize that threat, Hitler signed a German–Soviet Non-Aggression Pact—otherwise known as the Hitler–Stalin Pact—on August 23, 1939. This cynical agreement, accompanied by a separate trade treaty, appeared to be nothing short of an alliance between the two states and a division of northern and eastern Europe into German and Soviet zones. It was worse than it appeared. Part of the agreement was secret, and it constituted a pact made between ruthless men. Stalin would greenlight the German invasion of Poland, even as he prepared to assist Hitler by invading from the east. In exchange, Hitler accepted the Soviet invasion of Finland in the Baltic. The pact also involved large Soviet shipments of oil to Germany, and Communists around the world would be directed to immediately stop attacking Germany.

THE INVASION OF POLAND

With the elimination of the Soviet threat, Hitler wasted no time in authorizing *Fall Weiss* (Operation White), the master plan for the invasion of Poland. The assault opened at 4:30 on the morning of September 1, 1939, just a week after the signing of the German–Soviet agreement. More than 100 German divisions, a force of 2.5 million men, sped across the Polish border, where they were engaged by a Polish force barely one-tenth as large. On paper, the Poles had a reserve army of 3 million men, but most of them were under-trained and lacking good equipment. The German Blitzkrieg hit hard, with the Wehrmacht (German military) utilizing the most advanced tanks and planes available, while the Polish army carried out-of-date, even obsolete weapons. Some Polish cavalry met the enemy carrying only sabers and lances.

Britain and France had no choice but to respond. On September 3 both countries declared war on Germany. As for the Soviets, Stalin did not send his troops into Poland until September 17, but the result was the same. Poland was crushed by October 5. Hitler's assault on Polish soil had been so successful, in fact, that he altered the terms of his treaty with Stalin, offering him less Polish territory than they had originally agreed.

Today most historians consider September 1, 1939, as the beginning of World War II. Of course fighting had taken place years prior to that date in other parts of the world, with invasions elsewhere led by Japan, Italy, and Germany. The significance of September 1 lies in the fact that the German (and ultimately Soviet) invasion of Poland brought France, Great Britain, and its Commonwealth nations into war with Germany and her allies, thus increasing the scope of the conflict.

A WIDENING CONFLICT

With war now engulfing Europe, the U.S. policy of neutrality was being put to the real test. President Roosevelt was still limited in his responses by the neutrality acts, yet on a personal level he was far from neutral. He no longer had any intention of disguising his disapproval of the Axis powers and of his pro-Allies sentiments. For FDR, the Axis powers had to be defeated. Allowing Britain and France to fall was unthinkable, for U.S. security could not be guaranteed in the event of such a disaster. Roosevelt determined that he would take the United States into war before he would allow the democracies of the West to collapse.

But, even if the president had intentions of taking overt steps in support of the Allies, Congress was not prepared to follow suit without restrictions. Congressmen and Senators received an avalanche of hundreds of thousands of letters from American people who were concerned that the United States might enter the war. One such letter's message was clear and typical: "Keep America out of the blood business." Yet, Congress did amend the scope of the neutrality acts on November 4 with the Neutrality Act of 1939. The new act was a repeat of the 1937 act, with one important exception. This act repealed the arms embargo, so that the United States might be able to sell war materiel to the western powers. The act passed through Congress fairly easily. The 1939 act also empowered the president to recognize "combat zones," areas closed off to U.S. passengers and ships. (By 1941, this restriction was lifted to allow U.S. merchant ships sailing the Atlantic to arm and to allow such ships to deliver cargoes to belligerent ports.)

The Phony War

Additional steps soon followed. On January 3, 1940, FDR asked Congress to appropriate $1.8 billion for national defense, which included a program to build 50,000 new aircraft, which was considered a staggering number at that time. Such steps taken by Congress seemed almost too late as events that spring accelerated into high gear.

During the months immediately following the German invasion into Poland, things grew quiet across Europe. Despite France and Britain's declarations of war, no immediate fighting took place. The lack of fighting led some to dub the conflict as the "Phony War." The exception was the invasion by the Soviet Union of neighboring Finland on November 30, 1939, an effort designed to secure a strategic buffer territory between itself and Germany. The Finns fought bravely against the Soviet war machine, but, outnumbered, they sued for peace. By March 12, 1940, the Soviets had taken control of Finland and its government in Helsinki. They gained the territory they wanted but at great cost.

THE FALL OF FRANCE

The Phony War was shattered on April 9, when the Germans marched into Denmark, then moved north, capturing six major Norwegian ports along 1,000 miles (1,600 km) of coastline. The Danes were blown over, as their entire army numbered fewer than 14,000 men and their navy counted just two aged ships. Two days after the initial invasion, Germans occupied the Danish capital of Copenhagen. Norway soon followed and its capital, Oslo, was overrun. Then, at sunrise on May 10, the Germans launched *Fall Gelb* (Operation Yellow), as Blitzkrieg knifed into three small neutral nations—Luxembourg, Belgium, and the Netherlands. In just a few weeks, the German army had managed to invade and occupy five western European countries.

LENDING A HAND

Throughout the late summer and early fall of 1940, the British fought hard against the aerial might of the German Luftwaffe, exhausting the small island nation psychologically and financially. Britain's credit in America had just about been used up.

Roosevelt proposed a program by which the United States would not sell, but rather lend or lease war materiel to Great Britain and other Allied countries. The Lend-Lease Bill No. 1776 was titled "An Act Further to Promote the Defense of the United States." FDR waited until after his election in November to announce this plan, but his administration set out on a course of hard sell. They presented the alternatives in such tag lines as "Send guns, not sons" and "Billions, not bodies" to make the program more palatable to the isolationists. Roosevelt also touted his Lend-Lease proposal as one through which the United States would become the "Arsenal of Democracy," as U.S. weapons and other materials were sent to struggling victims of extremist aggression. Those nations would thus be able to continue their

This left France and Great Britain as the two remaining opponents to the Germans on the continent. There was no general panic among the Allies, for the French army was large, consisting of 5 million men. But when the Germans invaded in mid-May the French military fell apart. This was due in part to poor leadership from the French High Command, and in part to a policy established following World War I that relied on passive defense, embodied most obviously in the fixed fortifications along the northwest French border, known as the Maginot Line. This complex of anti-tank obstacles and underground bunkers had been built to meet the challenge of an advancing German army. These fortifications proved nearly worthless. The German invasion plan called for a roundabout attack from the north, through

difficult fight, without the United States needing to go to war itself.

The plan did have strong critics, including isolationists and Republicans who did not trust Roosevelt. The program seemed to represent nothing but a "blank check" to the Allies. Ohio Senator Robert Taft said what seemed clear to many others, that "lending" war materiel, including weapons, was like lending chewing gum: "You don't want it back." Congress passed the act anyway and soon one of the most ambitious federal acts in history was delivering billions of dollars worth of weapons and war vehicles to those fighting Germany, Italy, and Japan. It was, of course, by definition, as unnatural a move as the federal government had taken since war had broken out around the world.

Although FDR had labeled his program as an "Arsenal of Democracy," Lend-Lease materiel was delivered to China and the Soviet Union as well as to democratic Allies, such as Great Britain, Australia, New Zealand, and Canada. Through the next five years, a total of $50 billion in Lend-Lease materiel found its way into the hands of the Allies. However, the program did not manage to keep war from reaching the United States.

Belgium, not straight in from the east, allowing the German Wehrmacht to bypass the Maginot Line. In addition, German planes simply flew over the French defense system.

The Evacuation of Dunkirk

Aiding the French were tens of thousands of British Expeditionary Forces (BEF), who fought on French soil. Despite spirited fighting by the BEF, by May 21, 1940, they had been pushed back to the French port town of Dunkirk on the English Channel, with German tanks moving in for the kill. Evacuation was their only hope. Then Hitler ordered the Panzer commanders to wait until the German infantry caught up with them. This halt in the German advance gave the BEF time between May 26 and June 4 to evacuate.

In all, nearly 340,000 British and French troops were removed to England by 75 naval vessels, assisted by a flotilla of 850 civilian boats. Unfortunately, a great amount of British equipment had to be left behind, including tanks and other vehicles. The evacuation was constantly harassed by German Luftwaffe planes, as well as by German submarines (called U-boats) and E-boats (similar to Allied torpedo boats or U.S. PT boats). During the invasion of France and the evacuation of Dunkirk, the British government changed leaders, as Neville Chamberlain resigned on May 10, with Winston Churchill taking the reins as prime minister.

France is Occupied

The fall of France shocked everyone. Paris was in German hands by June 14. The city was spared throughout the Wehrmacht campaign as the French dubbed it an "open city," meaning it was left undefended. Meanwhile, troops defending the Maginot Line were largely unable to respond to the presence of German troops on French soil. The guns built into the line were fixed, pointing to the east, and it was impossible to turn them around to face Germans who were already occupying the country. Belatedly, on June 10, Mussolini declared war on France and Great Britain and launched limited invasion in southern France, with little territory gained. The occupation of France was completed on June 22, when French officials signed an armistice agreement. In a show of drama and dominance, Hitler forced the French leaders to sign the papers in the same railroad car in which German officials had signed the World War I armistice on November 11, 1918.

So much had been lost. The fight for France had ended with 90,000 French troops killed, 200,000 wounded, and 2 million taken prisoner or reported missing. The German losses were just short of 30,000 killed and 133,000 wounded. Hitler had accomplished the defeat of the nation that Germany had not succeeded in destroying during World War I. Only Great Britain now stood in the way of a complete German victory on the European continent. The scene was set for a major confrontation.

A CONCERNED ROOSEVELT

Back in the United States, Roosevelt was highly concerned about the turn of events that spring and early summer. On May 16, with the fall of France seemingly close at hand, Roosevelt went to Congress, asking for an additional $2.5 billion to further expand the nation's army and navy. Later that month the president introduced his Accelerated U.S. Defense Plan, which included a request for additional monies—$1.3 billion—to further build up the U.S. military. On June 22 Congress passed the National Defense Act, which appropriated nearly $1 billion annually while leaving room for even further additions to the national defense budget. Eleven new battleships, 50 new cruisers, and dozens of destroyers were to be built. Then, on September 6, Congress passed a conscription law—the first peacetime draft in U.S. history—which provided for the enlistment and training of 1.2 million troops and 800 reserve units annually.

THE BATTLE OF BRITAIN

With the collapse of the French in June, the Germans could begin focusing entirely on the downfall of Great Britain.

Pilots of Britain's Royal Air Force (RAF) run to their fighter aircraft to engage with German planes during the Battle of Britain. The RAF's victory delayed Germany's bombing and potential invasion of Britain.

From August through September, the British and German air forces shot it out in the skies over the English Channel, in a struggle known as the Battle of Britain. Holding out against the German air onslaught required nearly every available resource Great Britain had at its disposal. By the end of September, Hitler called off his air offensive, having suffered serious losses among his Luftwaffe forces. When the air war over England ended, the Germans had lost just short of 2,700 planes, while the British lost just over 900.

It was a singular triumph for the people of Great Britain and for Prime Minister Winston Churchill. With the failure of Germany's planned invasion of Britain, code-named Operation Sealion, and a defiant Great Britain still intact, the stage was set for the ultimate defeat of Hitler's forces. By the fall of 1940, however, the end of the war was not even close. Other nations, including the Soviet Union and the United States, had yet to join the conflict.

A THIRD TERM AS PRESIDENT

The events of the preceding year had profoundly disturbed large numbers of Americans. The result at home was a shift in the isolationist–interventionist balance. Countries in both eastern and western Europe had fallen under the harsh hand of Nazi rule. France had collapsed, and Americans sitting in movie houses across the country were stunned by the sight of Adolf Hitler and his High Command officers walking the streets of Paris nearly in the shadow of the Eiffel Tower. Roosevelt had stepped up his efforts to support those few nations still standing in the way of the German military machine. But he had to proceed with caution. It was an election year, and FDR had already served two terms in the White House. No president had ever campaigned for a third term. But he broke tradition, given his popularity and his party's general satisfaction with him as chief executive.

Giving a Helping Hand

The Republicans went to their convention that summer and selected as their candidate an Indiana lawyer of German descent who had until recently been a Democrat. An internationalist, Wendell Willkie appealed to the party mainstream as a man of honesty and integrity, even if he had little political experience. The Democrats wrestled with Willkie's campaign. He made an awkward target in some ways. He was not a blazing conservative, but a liberal who did not have a significant beef with the New Deal, except its price tag, its purchase of his electricity utility, and the meandering path it had followed over the previous eight years. Willkie spoke out against Roosevelt, accusing him of serving as a dictator of sorts during his years in the White House. The Democrats capitalized on Willkie's lack of political background (he had recently served as the head of a giant public utility corporation). One Democrat slogan defended FDR's third run for the presidency while back-handing Willkie's short political resume: "Better a Third Term than a Third-Rater."

Despite his intentions to walk lightly through the campaign, Roosevelt took a calculated and obviously uncharacteristic move that fall. At the request of Winston Churchill, early in September the president transferred 50 World War I -era, four-funnel U.S. Navy destroyers to the British navy, which needed them desperately to patrol the North Atlantic for German ships and U-boats. In exchange, the United States received eight strategic British air and naval bases scattered throughout the Western Hemisphere, from Newfoundland to South America. The United States would hold these bases under a lease extending for 99 years. The move was gutsy for Roosevelt, who made the decision to dispose of U.S. Navy property without consulting Congress. Isolationists howled in protest at FDR's non-neutral move and anti-Roosevelt Republicans joined the chorus.

With France, the Netherlands, and Denmark all under the Nazi boot, one concern Roosevelt had was the fates of some of their New World colonies. At the Havana Conference of 1940, Roosevelt agreed to share responsibility, along with 20 other nations of the Western Hemisphere, for upholding the old Monroe Doctrine. Rather than wield one-nation control over the Americas, FDR agreed to protect the "orphaned" European colonies and the nations of Latin America.

Willkie ran hard for the presidency. Busy with the mounting global crisis, FDR did not campaign much, gave few speeches, but did feel compelled to respond during a speech in Boston to Republican claims that he was pushing the United States into war, saying: "Your boys are not going to be sent into any foreign wars." Come election day, Roosevelt prevailed. The Democrats also kept power, retaining similar majorities in Congress that they had enjoyed going into the election. For many voters, it was more important to have a seasoned political veteran in the White House than to worry about a president serving three terms.

FURTHER STEPS TOWARD WAR

With his reelection behind him, Roosevelt began taking more aggressive steps in support of the Allies. He asked Congress for a Lend-Lease program, which became law in March 1941. Under this act, the president could "lend" war materiel to nations whose security and independence from extremist rule was considered vital to America's interests. Soon, billions in weapons, vehicles, planes, and other equipment were being funneled to fight the advance of Fascism.

The year was 1941, and the United States made no further pretense to being neutral in the expanding world war. Britain had become America's special ally, and Roosevelt did everything he could imagine to support the Anglo–American alliance. U.S. naval vessels patrolled the western half of the

Atlantic Ocean, so the British could keep their ships closer to home. Those same U.S. ships and planes fed a constant stream of intelligence data to the Royal Navy concerning the locations of German U-boats in the Atlantic. U.S. ports were open to British ships, yet through much of 1941, U.S. port authorities kept 65 Axis ships tied up in its harbors. Although the United States was not at war, some Americans were anxious to join the fight, so U.S. pilots joined the British and Canadian air forces, even as British pilots were sometimes trained at U.S. air bases.

Such non-neutral steps taken by the United States opened up the potential for direct conflict with the Axis powers. Several U.S. destroyers were fired on by German submarines, even though Roosevelt had made the decision to convoy U.S. ships across the Atlantic in July 1941. In September the U.S. destroyer *Greer* was attacked by a German submarine after trailing the sub, with little damage. After that attack, FDR ordered his naval commanders to fire on German warships on sight. In mid-October a German U-boat fired on the escort destroyer, *Kearny,* inflicting damage but failing to sink the U.S. vessel. Eight Americans were killed. Then, on October 31, 1941, a German U-boat sank a destroyer, the USS *Reuben James,* off the coast of Iceland, with the loss of more than 100 U.S. servicemen and officers.

By then Congress had removed the last of the restrictive neutrality laws, allowing armed U.S. merchant ships to deliver war goods directly to Great Britain, with permission to engage if fired upon. The result was heightened tension in the Atlantic. But it would be the Japanese, not the Germans, who would take the most decisive action against the United States, including a direct invasion on U.S. soil. December 7, 1941, would be the day that brought an end to the long-standing debate between American isolationists and American interventionists.

4

War Comes to America

The success of the German military in Europe also brought a change in Japan's war policy. With the governments of their mother countries under German occupation, the Asian colonies of France, the Netherlands, and even Great Britain, were tempting targets for the Japanese. (With Britain desperately defending itself during the summer of 1940 against German aerial invasion, its leaders had few resources to use defending colonial possessions.) The U.S. ambassador to Japan, Joseph Grew, warned: "The German military machine and their brilliant successes have gone to the Japanese head like strong wine." Grew's words were soon confirmed.

AN EMBOLDENED JAPAN

In mid-summer 1940 a new, hard-line Japanese government was formed, led by Prince Fumimaro Konoye. Strong, forceful men dominated the new cabinet, particularly the Minis-

ter of War, Lieutenant General Hideki Tojo, and the highly
ambitious Yosuke Matsuoka, the foreign minister. Having
attended college in Portland, Oregon, Matsuoka considered
himself to be an expert on the United States, which he did
not respect, believing its democracy made it weak and cor-
rupt. Soon the Konoye government was at work creating a
"New Order in Greater East Asia." Their plan assumed that
Germany would defeat Great Britain, leaving the British colonies in Asia defenseless against Japanese aggression.

As the new Japanese government developed its military
plans, the U.S. government became more concerned. U.S.
Secretary of State Cordell Hull distrusted the Konoye government; he was convinced the Japanese had sinister plans
for the future and would have to be stopped. Roosevelt
responded to Secretary Hull's concerns. At the end of July
1940 he ordered restrictions on shipments of U.S. scrap metal, lubricating oil, and aviation fuel to the Japanese, with the
intention of hampering Japan's ability to wage war.

New Plans of Aggression

The following month U.S. intelligence officials got a lucky
break, as cryptoanalysts deciphered the Japanese diplomatic
code. Named "Operation Magic," this breakthrough allowed
the U.S. government to secretly intercept and decode official
Japanese messages. While the messages were not specifically
about military plans, it was clear to Secretary of State Hull
that the Japanese were planning to escalate the war.

It came first in the widening of the Axis alliance. On September 27, 1940, the Japanese allied themselves with the
Fascist governments of Germany and Italy in a treaty called
the Tripartite Pact. While Japanese citizens at home cheered
the alliance, Japan began pursuing an even more aggressive
policy. With the Netherlands in German hands, the Japanese
pressured Dutch officials in the East Indies to sell them more

oil. With France under German control, French Indochina (modern-day Vietnam) gave the Japanese permission to land troops there, providing a jumping-off point for an invasion into southern Asia.

Unacceptable Terms, Fruitless Negotiations

To meet this challenge, President Roosevelt promised the Chinese leader, Chiang Kai-shek (today he is referred to more commonly by the Pinyin spelling as Jiang Jeishi), an increase in military aid, including $100 million in economic support, plus dozens of U.S. aircraft. America's arming of the Chinese angered the Japanese government, and Japan's political leaders called for talks with their U.S. counterparts. While negotiations did take place, they made little progress, and the rift between the United States and Japan widened further. Just as the Japanese had turned hard-line in Asia, so U.S. officials drew new lines in the sand, as well. Roosevelt said he would not reinstate oil shipments to Japan until it stopped fighting in China, removed its forces from Indochina, and dropped out of the Tripartite Pact with Germany and Italy. These terms were totally unacceptable to the Japanese, who demanded the United States stop supporting China.

The talks continued through the fall of 1940 and into the spring of 1941, as did the U.S. supply of oil to Japan. During these fruitless negotiations, the Japanese military was developing new plans of aggression. In early 1941 General Tomoyuki Yamashita began making operational a new strategy, which called for an invasion of Malaysia and the seizure of its capital, Singapore. The plan also envisioned an assault against the American-controlled Philippine Islands. Japan was still in need of more oil, so Yamashita's plan included seizing oil fields in the Dutch East Indies. Also, the general's strategy was determined to close off the only useable supply road into China from British-held India, the Burma Road.

This plan was bold and, to some Japanese military experts, frightening. Admiral of the Combined Japanese Fleet, Iso-roku Yamamoto, thought attacking the Philippines would open up the potential for war with the United States without doing enough up front to weaken America's military strength in the Pacific. Why not start the war in a way that would make Japan's chance of ultimate victory more likely?

Pearl Harbor Becomes the Target

By early 1941, Yamamoto had developed a plan of his own. He intended to strike at the heart of the U.S. military before attempting to seize the Philippines, which was occupied by a small force under the command of former U.S. Army Chief of Staff General Douglas MacArthur. Yamamoto's targets were the U.S. naval and air bases at Pearl Harbor, Hawaii. There, he hoped to cripple the U.S. Navy. His plan would require two aircraft carrier divisions to deliver the necessary number of planes; a destroyer squadron to "rescue survivors of carriers sunk by enemy counterattack"; one submarine squadron "to attack the enemy fleeing in confusion after closing in on Pearl Harbor and… to attack [U.S. vessels] at the entrance of Pearl Harbor so that the entrance may be blocked by sunken ships"; and "several tankers… for refueling at sea."

Like Japan's Foreign Minister Matsuoka, Yamamoto had spent several years in America and had even studied briefly at Harvard University. He had been the naval attache for the Japanese embassy in Washington, D.C. during the 1920s. He knew well the capacity of U.S. industry to manufacture war goods and other industrial materials. Yamamoto stated that Japan should not engage the United States in a war, because he did not believe his country could win.

Planning an attack on U.S. naval strength based in Hawaii was not an original idea. Nearly 10 years earlier Japanese naval officials had theorized about such an attack. In fact, every year throughout the 1930s all graduates of the Japanese Naval Academy were asked the same question on their final examination: "How would you execute a surprise assault on Pearl Harbor?"

Oil Embargo Leads to Crisis

The turning point in Japanese–American relations came on July 24, 1941, when Japanese forces, in defiance of the U.S. requests, formally occupied French Indochina. Roosevelt, convinced the Japanese had no intentions of holding back anywhere in Asia, declared an embargo on exports to Japan two days later. Now Japan would be unable to purchase U.S. oil, gasoline, metal, or other supplies necessary for continuing its expansion. Great Britain soon joined the embargo, followed by the Dutch governor of the East Indies. The Dutch had been selling the Japanese 1.8 million tons (1.6 million metric tons) of petroleum annually. With that supply cut off, the Japanese government faced a serious challenge. Supplies soon became extremely low and Japan was forced to ration gas and oil at home. In Tokyo, most of the taxicabs stopped running. Japan was in the midst of a crisis, with only enough reserves to last about 18 months. Something had to be done.

Events soon accelerated. Secretary Hull and President Roosevelt stood firm with the Japanese, insisting all their troops be removed from Chinese soil and that government officials sign a non-aggression pact with their Asian neighbor. Then, on October 16, Prince Konoye resigned from power at the insistence of the Japanese military. He was succeeded by the fierce and fanatical General Hideki Tojo. There now seemed little chance of avoiding a war between Japan and the United States. The oil embargo was considered an act of war by the Japanese military leaders, who were now firmly in power.

NEW HOSTILITIES AROUND THE GLOBE

As the Japanese prepared through the summer of 1941 to launch their attack against Pearl Harbor, the Germans took a bold step. On June 22, a year after the fall of France, Nazi troops invaded the Soviet Union. Soviet resistance was sporadic, and in some cases, completely lacking. Only the early snows of a Russian winter saved the Soviet Union from utter destruction. But, before the end of December 1941, the Soviet command regrouped and took the offensive, determined to remove the German menace from Soviet soil.

That same month, December 1941, witnessed the opening of hostilities and an expansion of World War II halfway across the globe. After months of planning, Japanese air and naval forces struck in a surprise attack against the U.S. naval, army, and air force installations on the Hawaiian island of Oahu. Admiral Yamamoto had succeeded in secretly steaming his vast fleet of ships and planes across the Pacific, until arriving only a few hundred miles off Hawaii. U.S. intelligence services had completely lost track of the fleet as early as November 16, even though the Japanese flotilla included 6 aircraft carriers, 2 battleships, 3 cruisers, 9 destroyers, 28 submarines, and 8 fuel tankers.

PEARL HARBOR

The Japanese attacked on Sunday morning, when many of the 50,000 U.S. servicemen stationed on Oahu were asleep in their bunks. Between 6:30 and 7:00 A.M. one of the Japanese midget submarines was spotted near the mouth of Pearl Harbor and sunk by the destroyer *Ward*. The ship's commander radioed in the details of the incident, but it was not immediately acted upon. The situation was under control. Meanwhile, at a radar outpost at Kahuku Point on the north side of Oahu, a giant blip appeared on a radar screen. It was the first wave of Japanese planes, headed toward the islands.

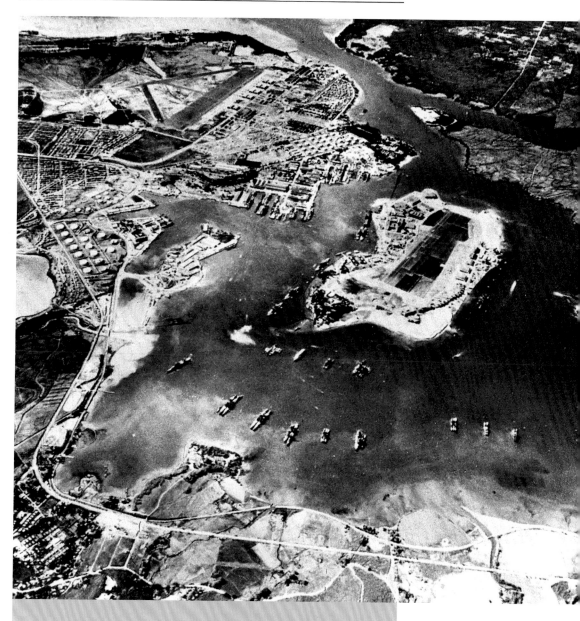

An aerial view of the U.S. naval base at Pearl Harbor, Hawaii, on the morning of December, 7, 1941, shortly before the Japanese attack. There were more than 90 U.S. Pacific Fleet ships anchored in the harbor— 21 were sunk or damaged in the engagement.

"A Date Which Will Live In Infamy"

The Japanese attack against U.S. military installations on the Hawaiian island of Oahu signaled the opening of true hostilities between the two countries. On Monday, December 8, 1941, President Franklin Roosevelt spoke before a joint session of Congress and requested a declaration of war against Japan. The following is his speech:

Mr. Vice President, Mr. Speaker, members of the Senate and of the House of Representatives:

Yesterday, December 7, 1941— a date which will live in infamy— the United States of America was suddenly and deliberately attacked by naval and air forces of the Empire of Japan.

The United States was at peace with that nation, and, at the solicitation of Japan, was still in conversation with its government and its Emperor looking toward the maintenance of peace in the Pacific.

Indeed, one hour after Japanese air squadrons had commenced bombing in the American island of Oahu, the Japanese Ambassador to the United States and his colleague delivered to our Secretary of State a formal reply to a recent American message. And, while this reply stated that it seemed useless to continue the existing diplomatic negotiations, it contained no threat or hint of war or of armed attack.

It will be recorded that the distance of Hawaii from Japan makes it obvious that the attack was deliberately planned many days or even weeks ago. During the intervening time the Japanese Government has deliberately sought to deceive the United States by false statements and expressions of hope for continued peace.

The attack yesterday on the Hawaiian Islands has caused severe damage to American naval and military forces. I regret to tell you that very many American lives have been lost. In addition, American ships have been reported torpedoed on the high seas between San Francisco and Honolulu.

Yesterday the Japanese Government also launched an attack against Malaya.

Last night Japanese forces attacked Hong Kong.

Last night Japanese forces attacked Guam.

Last night Japanese forces attacked the Philippine Islands.

Last night the Japanese attacked Wake Island.

And this morning the Japanese attacked Midway Island.

Japan has therefore undertaken a surprise offensive extending throughout the Pacific area. The facts of yesterday and today speak for themselves. The people of the United States have already formed their opinions and well understand the implications to the very life and safety of our nation.

As Commander-in-Chief of the Army and Navy I have directed that all measures be taken for our defense, that always will our whole nation remember the character of the onslaught against us.

No matter how long it may take us to overcome this premeditated invasion, the American people, in their righteous might, will win through to absolute victory.

I believe that I interpret the will of the Congress and of the people when

I assert that we will not only defend ourselves to the uttermost but will make it very certain that this form of treachery shall never again endanger us.

Hostilities exist. There is no blinking at the fact that our people, our territory and our interests are in grave danger.

With confidence in our armed forces, with the unbounding determination of our people, we will gain the inevitable triumph. So help us God.

I ask that the Congress declare that since the unprovoked and dastardly attack by Japan on Sunday, December 7, 1941, a state of war has existed between the United States and the Japanese Empire.

Congress took only an hour to approve the President's request.

When the blip on the radar screen was reported, it was falsely identified as a squadron of U.S. B-17s that were due in from California. All remained calm at Pearl Harbor.

At 7:48 A.M. the advance squadron of Japanese fighter planes, known as Zeros, crossed within sight of Kahuku Point. As the planes reached their target, the expanse of Pearl Harbor unfolded below them. Ninety-six naval vessels, comprising the bulk of the U.S. Pacific Fleet, crowded the docks and moorings of the harbor. Among the vessels were approximately 70 warships, including 8 battleships (one of the main targets of the Japanese), 30 powerful destroyers, 9 minelayers, 14 minesweepers, and 4 submarines. Dozens of additional support vessels—oil tankers, cargo ships, tugboats, repair ships, even a hospital ship—dotted the waters of the 8-square-mile (21-sq-km) harbor.

Seven blue-gray battleships were docked in two rows on the southeast of Ford Island, in the center of Pearl Harbor. Battleship Row, as it was called, was the prime target for the Japanese. One row of five battleships—the *California, Maryland, Tennessee, Arizona,* and *Nevada*—were docked almost bow to stern along the eastern side of the island. Two others—the *Oklahoma* and *West Virginia*—paralleled them on the left, or port side. The vessels were in such tight formation that escape was impossible. (An eighth battleship, the *Pennsylvania,* was also present at Pearl Harbor, but it was laid up in dry dock for repairs.)

"Air Raid, Pearl Harbor"

As the bombs began to rain down from the sky, an officer at the island's command center, Lieutenant Commander Logan Ramsey, dashed to the radio room, intent on informing as many of his fellow servicemen as possible that Pearl Harbor was under attack. At 7:58 A.M. Ramsey sent out a simple eight-word message on all frequencies in use in Hawaii:

The USS *West Virginia* and USS *Tennessee* are badly damaged by Japanese aircraft torpedoes and bombs in the attack on Pearl Harbor. Fires broke out on the ships, igniting the fuel and armaments they carried. The *West Virginia* soon sank.

"AIR RAID, PEARL HARBOR. THIS IS NOT [A] DRILL."

Japanese planes were soon filling the sky over the island, and, in minutes, the hanger and nearly three-dozen U.S. air-craft on Ford Island were on fire. The first wave of Japanese planes—including Zeros, high-levels, dive bombers, and tor-pedo planes, 200 aircraft in all—began pounding targets all across the island, from Pearl Harbor to the two army bases, Hickam and Wheeler.

The USS *Oklahoma* was one of the first battleships hit, a torpedo striking the ship's hull as the distant chime of church bells rang out eight o'clock. Additional torpedoes hit their target, and the *Oklahoma* began to list. Below decks, navy personnel were trapped. High-level bombers hit the ship's ammunition room, destroying the vessel, which began to roll over until her hull rose from the water, trapping 400 sailors in a darkened world in which up had become down. For those survivors on deck, the ship turned over so slowly that some men were rescued from the overturned ship with-out even getting their feet wet.

One after another, U.S. ships were struck, explosions rip-ping the Sunday morning calm. Nearly every large ship in the harbor was on fire by the time the second wave of 170 enemy planes arrived, an hour after the first wave had com-menced its attack. The second assault included 54 bombers that headed to Hickam Field and 85 dive-bombers ready to hit the ships at Pearl Harbor. Another 36 Zeros joined the fray. They soon saw the damage inflicted by their comrades.

The surprise attack on the U.S. installations on Oahu only took two hours. In that time, Japanese planes destroyed or seriously damaged 18 U.S. war vessels, including all 8 battle-ships. At least 160 U.S. planes were completely destroyed, and an equal number were damaged. By comparison, the Japanese lost just 5 midget submarines and 29 planes. The real losses of the day, however, were human lives. About 2,500 Americans were killed, including more than 2,400 U.S. sailors, soldiers, airmen, and marines. Another 1,200 Americans were wounded. The Japanese invaders only counted their dead at 64, while a midget sub's captain was the only captive taken by Americans.

As word of the invasion reached the Japanese public, the civilian population was ecstatic. They believed their military had carried out a great and honorable victory. In the United States, however, news of the attack infuriated the entire population. Up until late 1941, most Americans had opposed U.S. involvement in the ever-expanding war in Asia. Now they were prepared to fight a war of revenge against Imperial Japan. Politicians who had led the fight against U.S. involvement in World War II now made press announcements that the time for debate was over. It was time to go to war.

5
A Two-Front War

By the end of 1941 Franklin Roosevelt had already served more than two full terms as president. Less than a year of his third term had passed before he found himself leading the United States into a global war, following the Japanese attack at Pearl Harbor. The next four years would prove as challenging as any ever faced by a U.S. president. World War II was destined to become the greatest and most cataclysmic conflict in the history of humanity. World War I had brought the deaths of millions of individuals, soldiers and civilians alike, and destroyed centuries-old social and political institutions across Europe, including the colonial empires. But World War II was to create destruction, carnage, and absolute horror on a massive scale. In the end, it would alter the world in more ways, and more significantly, than any previous conflagration in history.

Most people in the United States experienced the war while removed from the violence by several thousand miles.

The domestic front was, in many ways, peaceful, with full employment finally bringing the Great Depression to an end. There were no bombings, no invasions following the Japanese attack at Hawaii, no massive upheavals of populations, and, while rationing of everything from gasoline to sugar became commonplace, Americans saw no serious loss of food or shelter. Yet, just as other populations around the world were changed by the war, so were the people of the United States, even if in ways that were not always obvious at the time. By the time the war ended, a new world lay ahead, one that was alternately filled with hope, as Fascism faced defeat, and fraught with challenge.

The attack at Pearl Harbor brought the United States into war not only with Japan, but with Germany and Italy, as well. Because Japan had signed an agreement with Germany and Italy, those two European nations declared war on the United States on December 11. The U.S. Congress responded immediately by declaring war on them. Thus the European and Asian wars had become one global conflict, with the Axis Powers—Japan, Germany, Italy and others—aligned against the Allied Powers, which included the United States, Great Britain, and the Soviet Union.

FIGHTING IN THE PACIFIC THEATER

Ten hours after the devastating strike at Pearl Harbor, Japanese airplanes attacked the U.S. airfields on Luzon Island in the Philippines, destroying much of the remainder of America's air power in the Pacific. Three days later Guam, another U.S. possession, fell to Japan, along with the American-held Wake Island, and the British-controlled coastal city of Hong Kong. During the weeks and months that followed, other dominoes fell in the Pacific, including British Singapore in Malaya in February 1942, the Dutch East Indies in March, and Burma in April.

On May 6 the Japanese overran American and Filipino defenders of the Philippines, who gave up their defense of the islands, including the holdout position inside the fortress of Corregidor in Manila Harbor. General MacArthur had already been ordered out of the Philippines by Washington officials and whisked off to Australia before the fall. Those who surrendered were taken prisoner and many were forced to participate in what became known as the Bataan Death March, an 80-mile (130-km) walk under bayonet guard to Japanese prisoner-of-war camps. Of the 75,000 prisoners involved, 10,000 or more were killed on the march.

Halting the Japanese Advance

Meanwhile, U.S. strategists began laying out a two-part offensive to turn the tide of war against the Japanese. Stage one involved U.S. forces under the command of General MacArthur, who would move north from Australia through New Guinea, bound for the Philippines. The second stage of the strategy would involve naval forces under the command of Admiral Chester "Chesty" Nimitz, whose forces would move west out of Hawaii toward major Japanese outpost targets throughout the central Pacific, taking each in turn, while shrinking the Japanese sphere of influence in the region.

The turnaround for Allied troops in the Pacific came somewhat quickly. That spring the Japanese invaded the turtle-shaped island of New Guinea, located north of Australia, then landed in the Solomon Islands. Their advance was finally halted during a crucial naval battle fought in the Coral Sea off the northeast coast of Australia in May 1942, the victory going to a U.S. carrier task force with assistance from the Australians. The entire battle took place, for the first time in history, between airplanes launched from aircraft carriers. The Japanese and U.S. fleets never came in direct contact with one another.

The Battle of Midway

The Japanese were undaunted and turned toward Midway Island, located 1,000 miles (1,600 km) northwest of Oahu Island. If the Japanese could capture this island, they could launch further attacks against Hawaii and, perhaps, even force the U.S. Navy to engage in highly destructive battles

Crew members inspect the aircraft carrier USS *Yorktown*, which was damaged by Japanese aerial and submarine attacks during the Battle of the Midway, June 3–6, 1942. The damage was so bad that the ship was eventually abandoned.

that might decide the war quickly. What unfolded between June 3 and June 6 would become the Battle of Midway, with Admiral Nimitz directing a U.S. carrier force against a larger Japanese fleet. Again, the fighting focused on airplanes seeking and destroying enemy vessels. When the Americans managed to sink four Japanese aircraft carriers, the cost was too high, and the enemy broke off the fight. (The United States lost only one carrier of its own.) The U.S. victory at Midway ended with several of the young Japanese pilots who had flown over Pearl Harbor on December 7 being killed during the fight. Midway represented more than just a singular victory, however. It marked the furthest extension of Japanese control in the Pacific. From the summer of 1942 until the end of the war, more than three years later, the Japanese were fighting a largely defensive war.

The Battle for Guadalcanal

During the months following the Midway battle, the Americans and their allies pushed hard against the Japanese in other theaters. When the Japanese reached to the north and captured two of the Aleutian Islands of Alaska—Kiska and Attu—U.S. commanders feared it signaled a new Japanese plan to invade additional U.S. territory from the north. One concern was the possible Japanese capture of the "Alcan" Highway that connected Alaska with Canada. Significant U.S. resources were dispatched to Alaska, but in the end, the Japanese reach in Alaska had already peaked.

With the initiative on their side, U.S. forces followed up their victories in the Coral Sea and at Midway with a campaign to break additional holes in the outer perimeter of Japanese control in the Pacific. In August, U.S. forces gained beachheads on Guadalcanal Island, located in the Solomons, in an effort to keep the sea-lanes between Australia and the U.S. West Coast open, while forcing the Japanese to yield territory. But the fight proved long and intense. After a time, the Americans began running short of supplies, only managing to hang on to Guadalcanal by a thread. The Japanese did not evacuate from the Guadalcanal region until February 1943, after suffering losses of 20,000 men. For the Americans, the losses had only risen to 1,700. Astonishingly, that ratio of casualties—approximately ten to one—remained the average of Japanese to U.S. losses for the rest of the war.

TARGETING GERMANY

Despite the fighting that unfolded in the Pacific Theater during 1942, much of the action involving the United States that year would be in the European Theater. Roosevelt and Churchill had already made a pledge to one another, the so-called "ABC-1 Agreement," in which both nations agreed to pursue the surrender of Germany ahead of all other goals—a controversial decision given the subsequent Japanese attack at Pearl Harbor. With many Americans clamoring to the U.S. military to go after Japan and seek revenge for the attack in Hawaii, FDR had to fight a popular hue and cry to pursue Germany first.

Yet this strategy was, in the end, the most logical. If the United States, through 1942, poured too many resources into defeating the Japanese, the Germans might emerge successfully from their fighting with the Soviets and British. This would cause the collapse of Europe, with the entire continent falling into Hitler's pocket. But with Germany defeated first, the Allies would remain together and would then be free to defeat Japan without distraction.

Roosevelt and Churchill had also made other agreements, even before the United States entered the war in December 1941. Four months earlier the two leaders had met on a warship off the coast of fog-shrouded Canadian Newfoundland. That August Churchill and Roosevelt worked out an

THEATERS OF WAR

World War II was certainly global. While fighting was largely contained within Europe, North Africa, Southeast Asia, and the Pacific Islands, countries from all over the world sent troops to support the main Axis and Allied powers. More than 100 million troops were involved and over 70 million people, the majority civilians, were killed in the war.

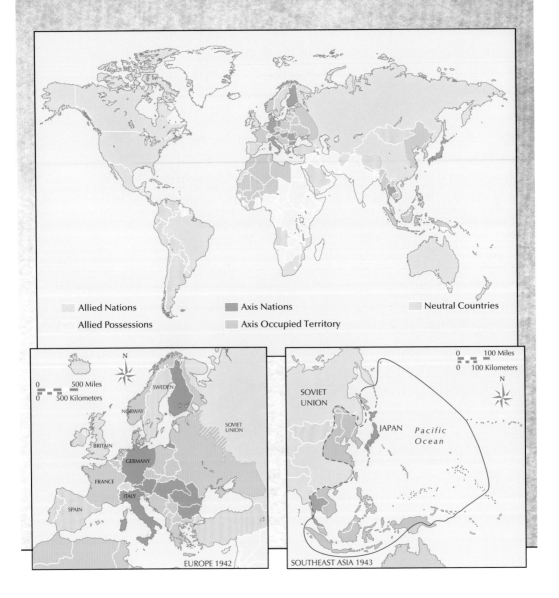

Allied Nations

Allied Possessions

Axis Nations

Axis Occupied Territory

Neutral Countries

EUROPE 1942

SOUTHEAST ASIA 1943

agreement they called the Atlantic Charter, an eight-point plan that vaguely recalled President Woodrow Wilson's 14 Points. In this document, the leaders of two of the world's most important democracies proposed that a goal of the war should be to establish a better world. To that end, the charter supported the right of self-determination for all nations. This meant that Great Britain and the United States (at some potential future date) would not be fighting to gain additional territory. The charter also stated that the rights of individuals, not those of nations, should come first. Additionally, the charter supported disarmament after the war was over and set out a plan for future peace and security, in the form of a "permanent system of general security." What the Atlantic Charter outlined in theory in August 1941 would eventually become the replacement for the old, ineffective League of Nations—the United Nations.

However, despite the ideals of the Atlantic Charter, the agreement was criticized by U.S. isolationists. The United States was not yet at war (Pearl Harbor was four months away). Why, then, was the president of a neutral nation agreeing to war aims with a nation already at war? The question might have been worth addressing, except for one glaring fact: The United States, by the fall of 1941, was no longer really neutral at all.

THE THREAT TO THE SOVIETS

The United States did not go to war with Germany and Italy without immediate problems. The country had not maintained much of a viable military between the two world wars, and only in recent years had the Congress funded great expansions of the Navy, Army, and Air Force. Therefore, the United States struggled to find stable legs in Europe through much of 1942. In the theater of war in Western Europe, the primary U.S. ally was Great Britain, but there was also support from the exiled "Free French" forces. Meanwhile, the other great ally of the United States was the Soviet Union, which had been battling hundreds of thousands of German troops since the summer of 1941.

Once the Americans came into the conflict in Europe, one overarching question was how quickly the Allies might be able to organize an invasion along the coasts of Western Europe and establish a major front. The U.S. commander, General George C. Marshall, believed such a plan—one calling for a major allied invasion of France across the English Channel—could be put together by the spring of 1943. To that end, he placed General Dwight D. Eisenhower in charge of the invasion landings in the Mediterranean in 1942 and in Sicily and Italy in 1943. In 1944, Eisenhower was moved to London to plan the Normandy invasion. As for the Soviet Union, Josef Stalin was intent on such a landing as soon as possible, because he believed his countrymen were bearing the brunt of the Nazi war machine on the eastern front.

THE SIEGES OF MOSCOW AND LENINGRAD

To say that the Soviets were coping with the war during 1941 and 1942 is a serious understatement. The German invasion into the Soviet Union had opened on June 22, 1941, and had involved nearly 3 million troops—a total of 148 divisions—along the long stretch of territory known as the Russian frontier. This huge force represented 80 percent of the entire German army, all backed by 2,000 Luftwaffe planes, 2,400 Panzer tanks, and 6,000 artillery pieces. The invasion had proved as devastating as Hitler had hoped. Air attacks had pounded the Russian defense troops. The Germans captured 300,000 Russians and seized 2,500 of their tanks. By September, the Germans had reached the outskirts of Leningrad and, by October, they were at the gates of Moscow.

The German sieges of these two cities were crushing on the civilian populations. After several months people in Leningrad were eating anything they could get their hands on. After eating all the animals in the city, including rats, they turned to consuming hair oil and Vaseline. They even made soup from the dried glue taken from furniture joints and from underneath wallpaper. Thousands of people died from a lack of food. In Moscow, the story was largely repeated, with 650,000 Soviet troops captured by mid-October.

Russian troops operate a gun emplacement in Leningrad (now Saint Petersburg) during the siege by German forces from September 1941 to January 1944. The Germans were finally expelled but not before some 300,000 troops on each side were killed.

SAVED BY THE WEATHER

But when heavy snows fell, the Germans were stranded, their tanks and trucks freezing up. Hitler had intended his Russian campaign to have been successful before that date, so German troops had not been issued winter clothing. The German supply line soon collapsed and the Wehrmacht soldiers were forced to eat their horses. By the end of November the Germans had 200,000 men dead and more than 500,000 additional casualties. The Russians launched a counteroffensive in early December and the Germans were pushed back, surrendering nearly all the territory in the Soviet Union they had gained during the previous six months.

But, despite the success of the Russian counter-offensive, the Soviets had suffered staggering losses. Of the 22,000 tanks the Soviets had in service prior to 1939, only 1,000 were still operational. Stalin's forces had counted 1 million casualties, plus 3 million Soviets taken prisoner. Then the Germans launched a new offensive in the summer of 1942. Stalin and the Soviet peoples were soon reeling under this new German advance onto their soil. It is not surprising, then, that the Soviet leader was calling loudly for the immediate establishment of a second front in Western Europe.

FIGHTING IN AFRICA

Following the attack at Pearl Harbor, FDR and Churchill met again the following month to establish a common strategy: to defeat Germany first. But the two leaders did not immediately agree on what steps should be taken. Stalin wanted a second front established in Western Europe, and FDR believed the Allies should launch an all-out attack across the English Channel before the end of 1942. But Churchill balked. He could easily remember the trench warfare of World War I that had stretched across the Western Front in France and Belgium, and he did not want this war to devolve back into those circumstances again. Churchill believed the Allies could launch a more effective front in North Africa.

The idea was a solid strategy. Churchill thought it important to attack the Germans where they were most vulnerable. By early 1942 German forces had infiltrated several North African nations. Also, the Germans were in the Middle Eastern nation of Syria and were preparing to push the British out of Egypt. Germany also had designs on Iran and Arabia, where there were rich oil fields. Churchill knew that securing these oil fields would be a vital victory for the Allies and a devastating loss for the Axis. He also believed the Germans were most vulnerable in North Africa and Southern Europe, including Greece, the Balkans, and Italy. An Allied landing along the southern shores of the Mediterranean Sea was planned, and General Dwight D. Eisenhower was placed in command of planning the landing.

El Alamein

Other actions preceded the Allied landing in North Africa. In May the British launched a 1,000-plane raid over the German city of Cologne. By August both British and U.S. planes were bombing additional German cities. Also in August, the British launched a commando raid against the French port city of Dieppe, largely relying on Canadian troops. The raid proved poorly planned and resulted in large numbers of casualties. But information was gained through the raid that was used in planning the eventual Allied landing on French soil, almost two years later.

Throughout the summer months the Axis tank units — Germany's "Africa Korps"—had driven across North Africa towards Egypt, under the command of Field Marshall Erwin Rommel, known as the "Desert Fox." In October Rommel was finally halted by British tank commander Bernard Montgomery at the Battle of El Alamein, west of Cairo, Egypt.

RELENTLESS ALLIED BOMBING

One of the longest campaigns of the war consisted of long-range bombing raids carried out by both U.S. and British planes against German civilian targets. By 1943 U.S. strategic bombers, alongside British bombers that had been hitting the Germans since the previous year, were flying almost daily missions, seeking any vital targets that might be of use to Germany, including factories, bridges, roads, and military installations. Such raids were eventually carried out both day and night. Initially, all the planes were flying from air bases in Britain but, once Italy was largely overrun in late 1943, U.S. bombers were flying from bases there too. Major German cities were targeted, with civilian casualties mounting with each attack.

U.S. planes were equipped during the war with a new device, the Norton bombsight, which was supposed to help bombardiers zero in on a specific target, such as a factory, while avoiding more innocent civilian structures, such as homes, schools, and hospitals. But the sight gained a reputation for being almost completely inaccurate.

With the constant bombing over many months, the Allied raids largely put German production plants out of business. Toward the end of the war, German oil production ceased and the railroad system was seriously disrupted so that it could not supply its army in Normandy. However, many German factories were still in operation and German manufacturing even managed to increase until the final months of the war. The raids did not even manage to bring about their secondary goal—the complete demoralization of the German civilian population. They did, however, deliver widespread damage.

The raids did accomplish one goal. The Allies had an almost inexhaustible number of bomber and fighter planes. Even though the German Luftwaffe managed to shoot down many planes, they were never able to match the number of enemy planes. As the war continued, the Germans were eventually forced to conserve both planes and pilots, leaving the Allies with some breathing room to carry out longer range attacks. This was made

U.S. B-17 bomber planes—protected by P-51 Mustang fighters—were operational mainly during the day and British bombers at night. As a result, U.S. bombers were more defensively armed and carried smaller payloads.

possible by another innovation of the war. Earlier, the flying range of Allied escort fighters had limited the distance bombers could reach on their missions. By the end of 1943, however, new jettisonable gas tanks allowed fighters to fly all the way to Berlin and back, leaving the German capital vulnerable. By 1944 the Allies had gained air supremacy.

With superior numbers and backed by hundreds of U.S.-made Sherman tanks, Montgomery pushed the German forces back to Tunisia, leaving Rommel more than 1,000 miles (1,600 km) from Egypt.

Operation Torch

On November 8, 1942, combined British and U.S. forces launched their large-scale invasion of North Africa, code-named "Operation Torch." Eisenhower had proven the man for the job. He was highly talented, daring, with a cooperative nature that other Allied commanders found reassuring. The landing was immense, including British and Canadian troops, French Resistance fighters, and a larger proportion of Americans. A flotilla of 850 ships was utilized for the invasion, even as thousands of Allied paratroopers drifted down from the skies into the North African desert. At that point in the war, the invasion represented the largest waterborne landing in history. Soon, the Germans and Italians were being pushed from both east and west until they were trapped in Tunisia, with the last Axis forces in the region surrendering in May 1943. Operation Torch was a success.

DECISIONS TO BE MADE

In the meantime, the Allied leaders had met again, this time in Casablanca, Morocco. Again, only Churchill and Roosevelt attended. Stalin had been invited, but had declined because his armies were still struggling against the German invaders, who were laying siege to Stalingrad when the conference was held in January 1943.

FDR and Churchill made significant decisions about their next moves in the war. They agreed to step up the Pacific war against Japan. They also envisioned their next major move in Europe as a campaign to cross the Mediterranean, using Tunisia as a springboard. From there, Allied armies would move to the island of Sicily, off the toe of the boot that was Italy. Once occupied, the island would provide a base for the next Allied invasion, this time to the beaches of Italy itself. With Allied troops in Italy, Churchill suggested, the Germans would be forced to redeploy divisions that might otherwise be stationed in France, which could leave France less occupied when a major landing was made there at a later date.

The "Big Two" made other decisions at Casablanca. They agreed to accept nothing short of the "unconditional surrender" of the Axis powers. This was intended as an assurance to Stalin and the Soviet Union that the British and Americans would never negotiate with Hitler or Mussolini to end the war and leave the Soviet Union hanging on its own. The agreement also meant there would be little possibility of an armistice, as had taken place at the end of World War I. At the same time, the "unconditional surrender" announcement made it clear to the Axis powers that the Allies were not strong enough at that point in the war to establish an immediate front in Western Europe.

ACROSS THE MEDITERRANEAN

The cross-Mediterranean strategy was underway by the summer of 1943. On the night of July 9, the first of 250,000 U.S. and British troops landed on the beaches of southeast Sicily. Under the command of the Allies' two top tank commanders—Generals Bernard Montgomery and George S. Patton—the occupation and subduing of Sicily took just over five weeks. Patton and his Seventh Army had reached the strategic city of Palermo within the first two weeks of fighting. Unfortunately, 40,000 German troops had managed to evacuate across the straits to Italy. With Sicily firmly occupied, the Allies were at Italy's front door, ready to invade Mussolini's mainland.

In the meantime, with pressures coming to bear, Il Duce's government had collapsed by July 25, and Mussolini himself was captured by Italian partisans. He was later rescued and whisked north to safety in Berlin by Hitler's top commando, Otto Skorzeny, who led a daring raid on Mussolini's hilltop hotel-prison. Hitler would then tell his Axis partner to return to Italy, where he set up a puppet government in the north. With the Italians unable or unwilling to stand against the Allies, Hitler sent eight German divisions into Italy, where they established a long and powerful defensive line south of Rome. By the first week of September, the Allies were landing on the beaches of the Italian peninsula—the main landing took place at Salerno—where they soon became bogged down in hard fighting and tenacious German defenses. With Rome as their objective, British and U.S. troops fought through the winter of 1943–44, engaging the enemy under some of the worst conditions of the war, including cold weather.

Italy is Knocked Out of the War

During the extended campaign in Italy that winter, Churchill and Roosevelt met again, and, for the first time, Josef Stalin was also in the room. The conference had almost not taken place between all three of the Allied leaders because Stalin was reluctant to leave Moscow and Soviet soil. However, once the location for the conference was set as Tehran, the ancient capital of Iran (formerly Persia), which shared a border with the Soviet Union, he agreed.

It was a risky trip for Roosevelt, whose plane entered combat air space on its way to the Middle East. On his way to Tehran, FDR stopped over in Cairo where he met with Churchill (without Stalin) to confer with the Chinese leader, Chiang Kai-shek. The result of the meeting was the Declaration of Cairo, through which the leaders of Britain and the United States promised to continue the war with Japan until its unconditional surrender, that all Chinese territory seized by Japan would be returned to China, and that "in due course Korea shall become free and independent."

Back on the mountainous battlefields of Italy, no real progress was made in the push toward Rome through the winter months, but the advance resumed in full tilt by May. On June 4, 1944, the Allies captured Rome, following months of fighting up and down Italy. Italy had been effectively knocked out of the war, but the Allied campaign had been won only through relentless fighting. Yet the victories enjoyed that early summer were eclipsed in just two days by the long-awaited Allied landing in France. D-Day—June 6, 1944—had arrived.

6

The Home Front

During World War II, while U.S. troops fought abroad in Africa, Europe, and Asia, the home front provided them with almost unlimited support. The old walls between isolationists and internationalists crashed to the ground after the surprise Japanese attack at Pearl Harbor. The war was, fortunately, removed from U.S. soil, which gave many a sense of detachment. The war was out there, somewhere, but only accessible through newsreels and newspapers, and the occasional letter that came from the servicemen and women in the field, which were highly censored by military officials, to make certain information was not accidentally leaked. Yet even as Americans did not have to contend with being bombed, life did shift into a different level of normalcy, as people, society, industry, and government moved into a wartime mentality.

There were those constant wake-up calls for hundreds of thousands of Americans stateside, when representatives of a branch of the military service showed up on a family's doorstep to tell them they had lost a loved one in the war. Throughout the four years of U.S. involvement in the conflict, 16 million men and women served in the U.S. military. This meant that almost one out of five families (18 percent) had a relative in the armed services. With 400,000 U.S. service personnel dying during the war, 180,000 children lost their fathers.

Another of those shifts on the home front was an expanding conservativism that lasted throughout the war. Despite high patriotism on the part of nearly all Americans, there was some discontent about circumstances, including price controls, restrictions on labor unions, and especially rationing. Even though Roosevelt had managed to gain a third term as president in 1940, the 1942 congressional elections signaled a change in the nation's political mood. Republicans gained 46 seats in the House of Representatives, representing a 10 percent shift in party balances. In the Senate, Republicans won nine seats, primarily from Midwestern farm states. Even though the Democrats did not lose many seats in the South, Southern Democrats in Congress turned more conservative.

A REVITALIZED ECONOMY

As for the remnants of Roosevelt's New Deal, the war dealt many of those decade-old programs a death blow. The New Deal, many thought, had served its purpose and needed to go. The Civilian Conservation Corps, the Works Projects Administration, and the National Youth Administration were all eliminated by Congress in 1942. Roosevelt himself cast off the mantle of "Dr. New Deal" and took on the cloak of, in his words, "Dr. Win-the-War." Government programs designed to battle the Depression were rendered unnecessary by the war, which brought full employment, better wages, and a revitalizing of the U.S. economy.

That economy boomed as never before. Between 1940 and 1945 the nation's gross national product doubled from $100 to $200 billion. Much of this increase was due, of course, to the war and its costs. In 1939 the federal budget had been $9 billion, and that was with the costs associated with the New Deal still in place. By 1945 the federal budget had mushroomed to $100 billion, an eleven-fold increase. The government spent a total of $330 billion during the war—twice the amount spent by the federal government during the previous 150 years combined! Compared to World War I, the costs of World War II were 10 times as high. At the peak of wartime production, the war was costing the U.S. government $10 million an hour.

CONSERVING TO WIN THE WAR

During the war, great efforts were taken by both the federal government and the American people to conserve precious resources for the war effort. As a result, many commodities were only available on a limited basis.

Rationed items included canned goods (cans required tin, which was in short supply and needed for war materials), rubber, gasoline, bacon, cheese, alcohol, coffee, shoes, sugar, meat, butter, and fuel oil. In some cases, rationing stamps were sold, allowing the buyer to purchase, for example, three gallons (14 liters) of gasoline a week. When the stamps were all used up, that person could buy no more gas until the next week.

The Office of Price Administration (OPA) introduced 10 major rationing programs by 1942, issuing rationing cards and coupons to more than 120 million Americans. The agency relied on the patriotic call to "Use it up, wear it out, make it do, or do without." The reach of the OPA was extensive, with sometimes unintended results. When the agency ordered a 10 percent reduction in the amount of cloth to be used in women's bathing suits, clothing producers cut out the middle, introducing an early form

All of this meant that the federal government continued its practice of deficit spending, which Roosevelt had begun in his fight against the Great Depression. The national debt increased accordingly, from $49 billion in 1941 to $259 billion by 1945. A large portion of that debt—$100 billion worth—was loaned to the Treasury through the sale of war bonds to the American people. Taxes were also increased, especially federal income taxes. The system was opened up so that four times as many people were paying into the system as before and Americans earning the highest wages were paying rates as high as 90 percent. To help the collection of these taxes, Congress enacted a withholding system of payroll deductions by 1943, a system that is still in place today.

of the bikini. Those who wore such swimsuits were showing not only their bare midriffs but also their patriotism.

Ironically, the order to ration and the call to conserve came at a time when many Americans were fully employed and making more money than they ever had. Unlike during the Great Depression, they now had money to spend, yet nothing to spend it on. Items such as gasoline were in short supply, and cars and houses were not available.

By 1942 the gap between average Americans' disposable incomes and the goods available for purchase came to a total of approximately $17 billion. By late 1944 Macy's Department Store in New York found many of its shelves completely empty. The previous year, retail companies began taking orders for goods that the buyers knew would not be available until after the war was over. In June 1944—the month of D-Day—General Electric advertised with the following promise: "Now we'll be glad to put your name down for earliest available data on postwar air conditioning and refrigeration equipment."

In the meantime, Americans put their hard-earned money in their savings account, a jar in the pantry, or under their mattress, in anticipation of the day when there would once again be goods to purchase in U.S. stores.

RETOOLING INDUSTRY

After a dozen years of a sagging economy, the war kicked U.S. productivity into hyper-drive, leaving the Depression behind. U.S. industry became responsible not only for supplying the needs of the U.S. military, but for producing endless war materiel for the Allies. Military orders were huge in scope, totaling $100 million just in 1942. There were those in America who were concerned about big business profiting excessively from the war, as had taken place during World War I. But Secretary of War Henry Stimson reminded those critics, notes historian Richard Abrams: "If you are going to try to go to war, or prepare for war, in a capitalist country, you have to let business make money out of the process or business won't work."

Just as the federal government had operated an agency to direct the wartime economy during World War I, so Roosevelt now established a similar government agency, the War Production Board (WPB), to oversee the production of almost incalculable levels of war materiel. Throughout the conflict, beginning in 1942, U.S. plants and factories churned out 40 billion bullets, 300,000 airplanes from fighters to bombers to cargo carriers, 76,000 ships, 86,000 tanks, and more than 2.5 million machine guns.

Production was almost all about the war. The WPB decided that automobile manufacturers should not make cars for domestic distribution, but war vehicles such as tanks and jeeps instead. With Japanese cutoffs of such essential natural resources as rubber, the WPB ordered the construction of more than 50 synthetic rubber factories. The government rationed many items, such as gasoline, tires, and food, while the nation's farmers were expected to produce as much as they possibly could. No one was now worried about overproduction on America's farms, as they had been during the Great Depression.

When inflationary prices hit in 1942, the government's Office of Price Administration intervened and reset prices. However, due to rationing, some Americans chose to pay more than the maximum price for some foodstuffs, such as sugar, butter, and meat. Just as prices were government-controlled, so the National War Labor Board set wage ceilings.

When the government seemed too heavy-handed in its control of the domestic economy and wartime production, some Americans responded by joining a labor union. During the war, union membership increased by 30 percent, from 10 to 13 million workers. When unions called for strikes several times over during the war, Congess passed the Smith-Connally Anti-Strike Act in June 1943 which authorized federal officials to order the takeover of any industrial plant or mine where a labor strike or work stoppage threatened production. Strikes in any government-operated industry were made illegal. Under Smith–Connally, the U.S. government took temporary control of coal mines and even some railroad lines. Union agitation and strikes, though, did not affect that many workers—perhaps 1 percent of the labor force. Great Britain, with the Nazi wolf sometimes knocking at the door, saw a higher percentage of workers strike than in the United States.

AMERICA'S WORKFORCE

World War II was a time of new opportunity for several different groups of workers in the United States, including women and blacks. During the war, the U.S. military oversaw more than 15 million servicemen, as well as 216,000 women who served in support and non-combat positions. Most branches of the service offered women an opportunity to wear a uniform, including the Army's WAACs (Women's Auxiliary Army Corps), the Navy's WAVES (Women Accepted for Volunteer Emergency Service), and the Coast Guard's

SPARS (an acronym taken from the Coast Guard motto "Semper Paratus, Always Ready").

Women at Work

Other women found jobs in factories and production plants. In all, 6 million American women worked outside the home, 50 percent of them for the first time in their lives. Since many of these women had children, government daycare facilities were set up, 3,000 in all nationwide. The factory jobs and industrial work offered to women knew almost no limits. Women could be found working in steel plants, welding metals, or operating heavy machinery. A common name for a woman who put her muscles to work in America's war plants was "Rosie the Riveter."

Some historians have, however, overemphasized the extent to which American women became commonplace in the nation's production plants. The vast majority of women, especially those married with children, remained at home. Many American females, when polled in 1943, stated they would not take a job in a war plant even if they had the opportunity. And, when the war ended, two out of every three female war workers gave up their jobs, some involuntarily, with the flood of returning GIs needing jobs themselves.

Workers From Mexico

With so many Americans donning military uniforms, some factories and farms struggled to find enough workers. In 1942 the federal government made an arrangement with the government of Mexico to allow thousands of temporary Mexican workers to come into the United States. Called *Braceros*, these Hispanic laborers were typically employed as fruit pickers and grain harvesters. Estimates put the number of legal Bracero laborers at 200,000, with another 200,000 likely coming to work illegally. The Bracero program proved so productive and popular with large farms that it continued for 20 years after the war was over.

The Bracero program was needed in such western states as California, even though the state saw an overall increase in population during the war of nearly 2 million people. This was part of a larger demographic shift for the West. Through-

"Rosie the Riveter" was a symbol of women workers during World War II. This poster was produced by the U.S. War Production Co-ordinating Committee.

out the 1940s the states west of the Mississippi River saw an increase in population of 8 million people. California led the pack, followed by Oregon, Washington, Nevada, Utah, Texas, and Arizona. Most of those new residents settled in urban centers. During the war years, San Diego increased its population by nearly 150 percent.

In such states as Washington and California, the incentive for much of the population increase was the number of wartime production plants operating within their borders. California production facilities alone received 10 percent of government defense contracts. In Seattle, shipyards and the Boeing aircraft plant brought an influx of workers, who arrived in such numbers that some Boeing workers had to live in tents temporarily, due to a shortage of housing.

OPPORTUNITIES FOR BLACKS

Minorities were a part of the mass migrations experienced in the United States during the war. The South saw some of the greatest changes. In 1944 mechanical cotton pickers came into use in the South, replacing the traditional stoop labor of blacks and poor whites. One reaping machine could do the work of 50 people, at a fraction of the cost. Blacks in large numbers were no longer needed to pick Southern cotton, a task they had carried out for 150 years. As a result, approximately 1.6 million Southern blacks left their traditional homelands during the war to find jobs in the West and the North, even though the federal government issued large numbers of defense contracts to Southern factories and plants. To man those factory jobs, nearly 1 million Americans migrated to the South from the Northeastern region of the United States. By 1944 approximately 2 million blacks were working in war factories.

Blacks across the country made important overall strides during the war. Hundreds of thousands joined the National

Association for the Advancement of Colored People (NAACP) to fight the latent segregation and discrimination remaining within the ranks of the U.S. workforce. Approximately 1 million black men served in the armed forces, in every theater of the war and in every branch of the U.S. military. They served, however, in segregated units, prompting one black soldier to observe, notes historian David Kennedy:

> Why is it we Negro soldiers who are as much a part of Uncle Sam's great military machine as any cannot be treated with equality and the respect due us? The same respect which white soldiers expect and demand from us?... There is great need for drastic change in this man's Army! How can we be trained to protect America, which is called a free nation, when all around us rears the ugly head of segregation?

Black servicemen were subjected to discrimination and petty racism, often relegated to menial jobs and denied combat opportunities. Even blood banks for wounded soldiers were segregated although, ironically, a black doctor, Charles Drew, had first developed the techniques used for blood transfusions. Several of the branches eliminated segregation in their officer candidate schools, but one exception was in the training of air force cadets. A flight school for blacks was established at Tuskegee, Alabama, which produced 600 pilots, lauded today as the "Tuskegee Airmen," several of whom flew in combat missions. The war gave many blacks opportunities, and many marched under the slogan "Double V," which referred to defeating dictators abroad and racism at home.

AMERICAN INDIANS DURING THE WAR

Among all the minorities in America, Native Americans may have supported the war effort more than any other group.

A "Tuskegee Airman" checks his fighter aircraft with two crewmen at Ramitelli airfield in Italy in March 1945. From this base, these airmen supported strategic bombers flying to Czechoslovakia, Austria, Germany, Poland, and Hungary.

Approximately one-third of American Indian men of service age put on a U.S. uniform. Another one out of four were employed in a defense industry. Indian women served as nurses or enlisted in the Women's Voluntary Service. To carry out their duties, many Indians left their reservations and soon gained new skills that made them more marketable after the war, even as they became detached from reservation life while adapting to life in mainstream U.S. society.

Motives for American Indians participating in the war varied. Patriotism appears to have been the primary reason. Despite their heritage of being mistreated by the federal government, many Indians felt they needed to help protect their homeland. Others joined the war because they had lost their jobs when New Deal programs were cut, so the war represented an opportunity to join the military as a replacement.

An Integrated Workforce

Some American Indian men went into military service to continue the tradition of their ancestors, with whom warrior societies had been extremely important. One Native American, Joseph Medicine Crow, recalled that during his service in Europe he did not make the connection between what he was doing and his tribe's warrior past. But, notes historian George Tindall: "[A]fterwards, when I came back and went through this telling of the war deeds ceremony, why, I told my war deeds, and lo and behold I completed the four requirements to become a chief."

While serving in the U.S. military, American Indians were not segregated as blacks were, but served in integrated units. One of the most important roles taken on by Indians was their service as "code talkers," in an effort to conceal information from the enemy. They were used to transmit radio messages, not using a special code but simply speaking their own languages to one another, which managed to baffle the

Germans and Japanese. Every branch of the U.S. military used Indian "code talkers," and the groups included Oneidas, Chippewas, Sauks, Foxes, Comanches, and, today the most famous, Navajos.

JAPANESE INTERNMENT

When the United States entered the war, patriotism ran at its highest level in decades. Unlike World War I, when German-Americans were almost persecuted, this war saw millions of German and Italian Americans jumping on the patriot band wagon, eager to support the U.S. war effort. A major difference from the World War I experience was that immigration to America had been dramatically reduced during the 20 years prior to World War II, so most European immigrant populations were already established here and had fewer loyalties to the Old Country. This meant there was little government or public harassment of those from countries with which the U.S. was now at war.

One exception, however, was with Japanese-Americans. Emotions ran high across the country following the Japanese attack on December 7, so Japanese living in the United States quickly became racial targets. Many lived on the Pacific Coast, especially in California. In all, they numbered close to 110,000, of whom approximately one out of three were naturalized, first-generation immigrants, called *Issei*. The remainder, known as the *Nisei*, were either naturalized or native-born citizens of the United States.

War Relocation Camps

In Washington, D.C., concern over the possibility of Japanese in the United States committing acts of sabotage led government officials to push President Roosevelt to issue Executive Order No. 9066. This forced the Japanese in America to be rounded up and placed in War Relocation Camps in such places as Arizona, Colorado, Wyoming, Utah, and Arkansas. Perhaps ironically, the 150,000 Japanese-Americans living in Hawaii were not included in the relocation. The U.S. military deemed their contribution to the islands' wartime economy too important to remove them, so their loyalty to America was not questioned.

Those who were sent to such camps typically lost their homes and their businesses, without compensation. Internees lost hundreds of millions of dollars in property and savings. When the executive order was challenged in the Supreme Court in 1944, the Court declared the act constitutional. The vast majority of Japanese people placed in such camps survived the war, but no compensation was made until 1988, when the U.S. government apologized to those who had been so callously abused and offered reparation payments of $20,000 to each of the 60,000 survivors.

Japanese in the U.S. Military

Following the attack at Pearl Harbor, Japanese-Americans who were already serving in the U.S. military were reclassified as "4-C, enemy aliens ineligible for the military." Many of them were relieved of their weapons and placed in segregated units, where they were allowed to do only menial work. *Nisei* who were members of the integrated infantry regiments in the Hawaiian National Guard were placed in such separated units by the summer of 1942. Ironically, more than 1,400 Japanese-American men had to fight to form the segregated "Hawaii Provisional Battalion," which first became the 100th Infantry Battalion, and later, the 442nd Regimental Combat Team.

By 1944, after being forced to live in relocation camps, Japanese-American men were subjected to the draft. When given the opportunity, 2,300 men enlisted straight out of the relocation camps into the U.S. military. The 100th Infantry

Battalion saw combat duty, but not in the Pacific Theater. They were sent to Europe, where they distinguished themselves in the fighting in Italy, taking heavy casualties during the battles at Monte Cassino. After engaging in 223 days of fighting, the men of the 100th Infantry Battalion and the 442nd Regimental Combat Team became two of the most highly decorated units in the history of the U.S. military. Japanese-American troops received 52 Distinguished Service crosses, 560 Silver Star Medals, more than 4,000 Bronze Stars, nearly 10,000 Purple Heart Medals, and 7 Presidential Unit Citations.

It was in no small part due to the contributions made by such minority military units during World War II as the Tuskegee Airmen, the 100th/442nd Regimental Combat Team, the American Indian Code Talkers, and the 1st/2nd Filipino Infantry Regiment that, following the war, President Harry Truman made the decision to sign Executive Order No. 9981, which brought about the desegregation of the U.S. military in 1948.

7
Victory for the Allies

By mid-1943 the Allies, led by the Americans, with support mainly from the Australians and New Zealanders but also some Dutch colonials, had achieved a shift in the initiative concerning the war in the southern and central Pacific. In fact, the Japanese advance had been stymied through hard fighting at several points along the Japanese perimeter of control and the Allies had now taken the offensive. But the war was not nearly over. Some of the toughest fighting lay ahead over the next two years. Yet, ultimately, the war in the Pacific would not end as anyone could have predicted at that mid-point of the war.

OPERATION OVERLORD

Meanwhile, in the European Theater, Allied armies were preparing to finally launch their offensive to establish a Western European front. Constant air bombing missions had struck against German targets month after relentless month so that, by early 1944, major German cities including Leipzig, Cologne, Hamburg, and Berlin had either been devastated or damaged extensively. In mid-February a series of major air attacks against the German city of Dresden had taken place in which 1,300 British and U.S. planes had flown over the town in four separate bombing raids. Dresden was the home of over 100 factories, where 50,000 German workers manufactured war materiel for the Third Reich. The bombings of February 14–15 involved incendiary bombs that created a great firestorm. This destroyed 75 percent of the previously undamaged parts of the city, and killed between 25,000 and 45,000 civilians.

Preparations on Both Sides

Such raids were intended to hasten the end of Germany's capacity to wage war. Still, Allied military leaders understood the necessity of creating a Western European front. For two years an enormous offensive force had been assembling in Great Britain, including 3 million troops and a vast array of naval vessels carrying huge numbers of armaments. Under the leadership of the U.S. general, Dwight D. Eisenhower, the armada slated to establish beachheads along the coast of France's Normandy was the greatest such force ever brought together in one place during wartime. By the morning of June 6, 1944, this mega-invasion force was ready to be put into action.

During those years of planning, the Germans had been busy establishing their defense of the Normandy coastline. Captured European workers had been forced to build fortified and reinforced concrete blockhouses, called pillboxes, to house German artillery and machine gun placements. The beaches had been littered with 4 million landmines, plus endless miles of barbed wire and antitank obstructions fashioned out of multiple steel girders. So much preparation had gone into the German defenses at Normandy that Eisenhower's plan for the invasion only stood a 50 percent chance of success.

On June 5, the evening before the assault, Eisenhower visited with 16,000 U.S. paratroopers, who assured him they would do their duty. Eisenhower returned to his staff car, his eyes welling with tears. He knew the next 24 hours would prove crucial to the outcome of the war. He also understood that many of those young men he had spoken to would likely be killed over the next several days or even hours. As for the Germans, their commander in Normandy, Field Marshal Erwin Rommel, had left France on June 4, bound for Berlin. He had become convinced that no invasion was going to take place and that, if it did, it would definitely fail.

ON TO THE BEACHES

At dawn on June 6—D-Day—Operation Overlord swung into action. Amphibious landing craft delivered 150,000 men to the beaches of Normandy, including 57,000 Americans, along with British and Canadian troops. They surprised the German defenders, who were convinced the invasion would take place 200 miles (320 km) away to the northeast, at the medieval port of Calais.

The landing at Normandy would prove a success, but it was not without mistakes and glitches. Many of the paratroopers landed in the wrong places, due to overnight cloud cover. Bombardment of German coastal defenses proved largely ineffective. More than 1,000 Allied troops drowned when high waves capsized landing crafts. Radios did not work, mostly because of water damage. Confusion reigned on the beaches. At Omaha Beach, U.S. troops met their greatest resistance, coming under heavy crossfire from German positions along the cliff sides. In one 10-minute timeframe, one U.S. rifle company suffered 197 casualties among its 205 members. By the end of D-Day, the Allies had suffered 5,000 casualties, including the killed and wounded. But, despite the high numbers of Allied losses, the Germans sustained even greater numbers of casualties. D-Day was a success.

Over the next two weeks, the Allies kept landing men until the number reached 1 million. The landing at Normandy so thoroughly routed the Germans that Field Marshal Rommel became convinced that the war was lost and soon became embroiled in an unsuccessful plot to assassinate Hitler on July 20. For his disloyalty, Rommel was allowed to commit suicide.

U.S. soldiers unload from a landing craft at Utah Beach in Normandy during the invasion of France that started on June 6, 1944.

The Liberation of France

Slowly, but methodically, Allied armies advanced from the beaches of Normandy. In late July, during the battle of Saint-Lo, U.S. General Omar Bradley's First Army broke through German lines. General George Patton's Third Army, with his tanks spearheading the assault, filled the hole created by Bradley's men, as they drove into the heart of France. On August 15 a joint U.S.–French invasion force landed along the coast of Southern France and began moving up the Rhône Valley against inadequate German resistance. Paris was liberated by Free French forces on August 25, more than four years since its occupation by the Nazis.

By mid-September 1944 the Allies had driven nearly all German forces out of both France and Belgium. However, the Allied armies' drive came to a halt along the western banks of the Rhine River, where desperate German forces laid down a line of defenses, determined to keep the Allies from crossing into Germany itself. During the next couple of months, cold weather set in and the fighting was dramatically reduced in scale.

THE BATTLE OF THE BULGE

Back in the United States, President Roosevelt was in the midst of his fourth campaign for the presidency. Roosevelt, who had been president for nearly 12 years and was showing the signs of fatigue, exhaustion, even ill health, won another election. It appeared Roosevelt would see the war through as the nation's longest-serving president.

But the war in Europe was at a standstill. Then, in the dead of a harsh December winter, the Germans launched a massive offensive through the Ardennes Forest in Belgium and France. They surprised the Americans where they appeared to be the thinnest and pushed them back along a 50-mile (80-km) front in Belgium and Luxembourg until they were finally halted at the Belgian town of Bastogne. The Battle of the Bulge would prove to be the last major German offensive of the war. The fighting centered around the U.S. defense of Bastogne, where German forces surrounded the town.

For six days U.S. troops fought tooth and nail in the snow. On December 22 the Germans demanded the surrender of the U.S. commander inside Bastogne, General "Tony" McAuliffe. His reply was "Nuts!," but little hope remained for McAuliffe and his army until the weather changed and the skies were cleared of clouds, which allowed Allied planes to drop supplies to the defenders of Bastogne and bomb German positions. By December 26, Bastogne was liberated, yet the Battle of the Bulge would continue until mid-January, when the Germans were finally dislodged from the ground they had gained and the previous lines that had been in place before the German offensive were restored.

CLOSING IN

As 1945 opened the Allies were advancing across Germany from nearly all directions. Hitler had used up his last reserve forces on his Battle of the Bulge gambit and his nation lay largely exposed, ripe for the Allied taking. The British had already launched "Operation Market Garden," in which British commander Bernard Montgomery attacked through Belgium and the Netherlands, trying to cross river bridges into the Ruhr, the industrial heartland of Germany. The mission failed: It was later referred to as "a bridge too far." Meanwhile, the Soviets were sweeping across Central Europe and the Balkans and, by late January, launched a great offensive toward the Oder River inside Germany. By early spring they were preparing to launch their final assault against the symbolic heart of Germany—Berlin.

At the same time, General Omar Bradley was advancing with his First Army toward the Rhine River from the west. In early March his men captured the German city of Cologne, nestled on the Rhine's west bank. The following day some of Bradley's men made a miraculous find: an undamaged bridge crossing the Rhine at Remagen. Soon Allied troops were converging on the bridge and pouring across the river.

SURVIVORS OF THE "FINAL SOLUTION"

As they advanced, the Allies stumbled upon concentration camps run by the Nazis, where millions of "undesirables" had been killed. The majority of the victims were Jews, the ethnic minority that Hitler had repeatedly targeted for 12 years. Allied troops found some of these barbed wire enclosures still holding their skeletal inmates, survivors of Hitler's "Final Solution."

FDR and other federal government officials had known of these camps and the Jewish Holocaust they represented since the early 1940s, but, along with other Allied leaders, had taken no overt steps to liberate the captives or at least destroy the facilities. Allied leaders had not even authorized the bombing of rail lines leading to the camps, which might have deterred the Germans from delivering additional victims to their deaths. To an extent, Allied leaders did not understand the scope of the Nazis' extermination program prior to the liberation of these camps. But the horrors became reality to them and the world during these final months of the war. Historians believe the Nazis exterminated 6 million Jews and 4 million others, including Slavs, Gypsies, and Poles.

THE END OF THE WAR IN EUROPE

During the weeks that followed, the Allies tightened the noose around the neck of the Nazis. Montgomery reached Germany from the north, backed by 1 million men. Meanwhile, Bradley's forces completely encircled 300,000 German troops in the Ruhr Valley. Caught between the British to the

North, the Americans in the West, and the Russians advancing from the East, German resistance buckled and broke.

Yet, in the midst of the collapse of Germany, Winston Churchill was increasingly concerned about whether Soviet troops should be allowed to reach Berlin first. From such a geographic position of strength, Stalin might be able to dictate the final terms of surrender in his favor. Churchill

LIBERATING THE CONCENTRATION CAMPS

Russian troops were the first to encounter and liberate inmates from German concentration camps, starting in July 1944. The first camp liberated by U.S. forces was at Buchenwald on April 11, 1945. Soon after, they liberated four more major camps. The first major camp liberated by British troops was Bergen-Belsen in mid-April 1945.

U.S. troops try to help survivors of a concentration camp. All the survivors were weak and malnourished; many continued to die after liberation.

approached FDR, asking him to step up U.S. movements toward Berlin, but the president, who was struggling with declining health, left the decision to his field commander, General Eisenhower. When Eisenhower asked General Bradley what it would cost to take Berlin ahead of the Russians, he was told it might result in 100,000 casualties. Eisenhower then made his decision, stating the losses represented a "pretty stiff price to pay for a prestige objective [Berlin]." The Supreme Commander of Allied Forces decided to leave the capture of Berlin to the Russians.

The Deaths of Two Leaders

By April 1945 the Soviets were on the outskirts of Berlin, where Adolf Hitler and his loyal entourage had taken refuge in a bunker more than 26 feet (8 m) beneath the garden of the old Chancellery building. The Soviets had to fight door-to-door through the city; they killed everyone who resisted, and engaged in wholesale pillage and rape. As for the German leader, Hitler quickly married his longtime mistress, Eva Braun, then committed suicide in his bunker on April 30. Many of those within the bunker, including the wives of those in Hitler's entourage, also killed themselves, but not until they had given poison to their children.

By this time President Roosevelt himself was already dead, having collapsed with a cerebral hemorrhage on April 12 at Warm Springs, Georgia, where he regularly visited the mineral baths. For more than 12 years, FDR had led Americans through the dual national challenges of the Great Depression and World War II. Young people across the United States, including those in high school, had never known a time when Franklin Delano Roosevelt was not the president. His passing was mourned across the nation much as the nation had mourned President Lincoln at the end of an earlier American war.

The Germans Surrender

During the week following Hitler's suicide, tentative representatives of the German government sent out feelers, intending to surrender. On May 7 that surrender was accepted unconditionally. The following day was officially proclaimed as V-E Day (Victory in Europe). Millions of troops and hundreds of thousands of civilians across Europe had died during the previous six years of war. But, at last, the conflict was ended and Hitler's Fascism had perished in the burned-out rubble of Berlin.

THE FALL OF THE BAMBOO EMPIRE

The spring of 1945 signaled the end of the war in Europe, but the conflict in the Pacific between the Japanese and the Allies would continue for another four months. Through 1943 and 1944 the Allies had remained on the offensive, engaging in "leap-frogging" across the Pacific, with each military victory placing the Allies closer to Japan itself. Despite taking ten times as many casualties as their opponents, Japanese soldiers proved hard fighters who refused to surrender, sometimes choosing suicide instead.

In 1944 the scales tipped unalterably for the Allies, as General MacArthur's forces drove the Japanese from the northern coast of New Guinea, northeast of Australia. This represented a crucial breakthrough point along the furthest perimeter of Japanese control in the Pacific. During the previous 12 months, Allied armies had pushed the Japanese out of the Aleutian Islands, the Gilbert Islands, and the Marshall Islands. In the Marianas, the fight for Guam ended with the loss of 250 Japanese planes and only 29 U.S. planes, thanks in part to a new U.S. fighter plane, the "Hellcat." The capture of Guam provided a base for the new U.S. B-29 super bombers, which were capable of launching air attacks on Japan's home islands. These raids opened in June 1944, just weeks following the successful Allied landing at Normandy on D-Day. At the same time, U.S. naval forces sank several Japanese aircraft carriers in the Battle of the Philippines, losses the Japanese could not replace and from which they would never recover. By November 1944 Allied bombing raids on Japan were taking place around the clock.

Destruction of the remnants of the Japanese empire was the order of the day. U.S. submarines sank more than 1,000 Japanese merchant vessels (half of their trade fleet) as planes bombed Tokyo and other Japanese cities with firebombs. On March 9–10 a massive raid nearly leveled the Japanese capital from the air, destroying 250,000 buildings, leaving a quarter of the city in ruins and 83,000 people dead.

Yet the Japanese did not consider surrender, even following the Battle of Leyte Gulf—a combined air and naval battle that unfolded during October 23–26. Actually a series of three battles, the fighting at Leyte left the Japanese navy crushed, with 60 ships destroyed. Those Japanese vessels still afloat in the Pacific now faced more than 4,000 Allied naval vessels, including some of the battleships that had been heavily damaged during the attack on Pearl Harbor nearly three years earlier. Following the success at Leyte, the Allies hit the beaches at Luzon, the main Philippine island, in January 1945, against hard Japanese resistance that claimed more than 60,000 U.S. casualties.

Iwo Jima

The next target for the Allies was Iwo Jima, a tiny Pacific island situated south of Japan. The land assault on the island was preceded by 72 days of aerial attacks, during which 5,800 tons (5,300 metric tons) of bombs were dropped. On February 19, 1945, 30,000 troops of the 4th and 5th marine divisions stormed the island's beaches. Within a few days, more than 75,000 marines had landed on Iwo Jima. The fighting on the tiny volcanic island dragged on for 36 days of continuous ground combat, involving the landing of 110,000 men, backed by double that number of sailors, marines, and soldiers who remained offshore on 800 warships. By mid-March Iwo Jima was securely in U.S. hands. While the battle

A group of U.S marines of the 5th division plant the "Stars and Stripes" on top of the hard-won Mount Suribachi on Iwo Jima Island, Japan, on February 23, 1945. The photograph was taken by Associated Press photographer Joe Rosenthal.

ended in a U.S. victory, it cost about 24,000 U.S. casualties, including 5,900 dead. But the noose was tightening round Japan. From a new U.S. base on the island, planes flying back from raiding the Japanese mainland could make emergency landings.

Okinawa

While Iwo Jima was 750 miles (1,200 km) from Tokyo, the islands of Okinawa were only half that distance away. On April 1, Okinawa became the new scene of concentrated fighting, involving the largest amphibious assault of the Pacific War. In all, hundreds of thousands of troops participated in the action on Okinawa. The fighting extended on for six weeks of brutal combat and revealed the strength of Japanese resistance.

Running parallel to the fight at Okinawa were repeated missions carried out by Japanese zealots called kamikazes— pilots who flew planes filled with explosives and crashed them into Allied ships, an act of *hara-kiri* (suicide) carried out in the name of Japan's god-like emperor. In all, 3,500 kamikaze flyers caused great damage on U.S. and British vessels, resulting in the sinking of 30 ships and the damaging of dozens of others. When the Allies finally broke Japanese resistance on Okinawa, 100,000 Japanese soldiers had died. Allied losses were 37,000 wounded and 12,500 dead.

A Change of Plan

The fight for Okinawa resulted in more than 250,000 casualties on both sides. Japanese resistance had proven as strong as ever, but the curve was shifting ultimately in favor of the Allies. Japan had almost no ships or planes left with which to continue the war. Tokyo had been firebombed; home island morale was low. U.S. officials were aware that Japanese leaders had reached out to the Soviet Union with peace feelers, since that country was not directly at war with Japan. Yet most leaders could not imagine Japan simply giving up, regardless of its true incapacity to continue the fight for much longer.

THE MANHATTAN PROJECT

During World War II several new technologies came into use that altered the scope and nature of modern warfare, including such innovations as sonar, rockets, and jet planes. But none of these had a more dramatic effect than the atomic bomb.

Reports began reaching the United States in 1939 that Nazi scientists had taken the initial steps in creating an atomic weapon, one more powerful than any military technology that had ever existed. That year Albert Einstein, who had fled from Germany during the 1930s, sent a letter to President Roosevelt in which he suggested the possibility of developing an atomic bomb. FDR, uncertain how to proceed, authorized only $6,000 in February 1940 for a study on the feasibility of such a technology. In 1942 the fledgling program was put in the hands of the War Department, and by mid-year researchers concluded that using fission to create a military weapon was possible, but would be extremely expensive.

Soon, the Americans, British, and Canadians began working on a joint program to create an atomic bomb. As some of the early research had taken place at Columbia University in Manhattan, it was referred to as the Manhattan Project. Its purpose: To develop an atomic device before the Germans did it first. An atomic weapon would hold such power that whichever nation developed it first would be able to force terms on its enemies and emerge from the war victorious.

Over the next three years work continued under strict secrecy and security. Every facility had to be built from scratch, including those in Los Alamos, New Mexico, and Oak Ridge, Tennessee. General Leslie R. Groves, an army engineer, was put in charge of overseeing the building of these facilities. Groves had just

The invasion of Japan had been on the drawing boards of military strategists for months. All involved believed that an all-out invasion of the Japanese Islands would result in hundreds of thousands of Allied casualties, perhaps as many

completed work on the construction of the Pentagon, the army's new headquarters, then the largest office building in the world. Rumors flew that not only the Germans were working on such a weapon, but that the Soviets and the Japanese were also busy with similar projects. In fact, each nation did have a sizeable atomic program, but none of them made real progress. The Los Alamos laboratory opened in 1943, and research was headed by an American physicist named J. Robert Oppenheimer.

By 1945 the scientists had produced a prototype weapon ready to test in the field. The basic technology was designed to create a sustained explosive chain reaction by bringing together enough fissionable material to create what the scientists called a "supercritical mass." But everything remained theoretical until a test was performed. The physicists at Los Alamos chose a remote location in New Mexico called Alamogordo, 120

miles (193 km) south of Albuquerque. The site was code-named Trinity.

At 5:30 A.M. on July 16, 1945, the test device, suspended from a metal tower, was detonated. Before this first atomic bomb was exploded, the scientists had no clear concept of how large the explosion would be or even if the device would explode at all.

For the first time in history, the world witnessed an atomic explosion. The device lit up the night sky with an illumination that could be seen 180 miles (290 km) away. At the detonation site, the tower was completed destroyed as the bomb's core reached a temperature of 60 million degrees, turning New Mexico desert sand into an eerie green glass. A great mushroom-shaped cloud rose from the site to a height of 40,000 feet (12,000 m).

As Oppenheimer witnessed the blast, he was dumbfounded, and a line from a Hindu Sanskrit text came into his mind: "I am become Death, the destroyer of worlds."

as 1 million. In July 1945 President Harry Truman met with Churchill and Stalin (Churchill was voted out of office during the conference and was replaced by a new prime minister, Clement Attlee) at Potsdam, Germany, for 17 days. The Big Three issued an ultimatum to the Japanese: surrender or face annihilation. However, during this conference Truman received a message that would alter the end of the war and eliminate the need for a full-scale invasion of the Japanese mainland: The world's first atomic bomb had been successfully detonated at a testing site near Alamogordo, New Mexico.

Hiroshima and Nagasaki

Truman, who had only gained the presidency three months earlier, now had a momentous decision to make—whether to use an atomic bomb against Japan in the hopes the Japanese would sue for peace and bring the war to an abrupt end. The Potsdam ultimatum of "surrender or face destruction" was soon delivered. Informed that the United States had a devastating weapon at its disposal, Japanese leaders still refused to capitulate. On August 6, 1945, world history was forever altered when a U.S. bomber plane, a B-29 named *Enola Gay,* dropped an atomic bomb on the Japanese city of Hiroshima. The detonation instantly killed 70,000 people, nearly all of whom were civilians. The bomb's mushroom cloud, the intense heat, and the radiation release represented nothing ever seen in war before. A further 60,000 victims would die later from burns and radiation disease.

Despite the devastation unleashed by this first bomb, the Japanese refused to surrender. Two days later Stalin announced the Soviet Union was entering the war against Japan, a calculated move. The following day, August 9, a second atomic bomb was dropped, this time on the Japanese city of Nagasaki, killing another 80,000 people. This marked the end of the war and the capitulation of the Japanese will to continue fighting.

On August 10, 1945, officials in bombed-out Tokyo sued for peace, with only one condition: That their emperor, Hirohito, be allowed to keep his ancestral throne as a ruler with reduced power. Although the Allied leaders had always

The aftermath of the atomic bomb on Hiroshima. The bomb was dropped by parachute and exploded 1,888 feet (580 m) above the city. More than 60 percent of the buildings were totally destroyed.

called for the unconditional surrender of Japan, they agreed to this single stipulation, accepting the Japanese request on August 14. Nearly three weeks passed before the official surrender ceremony.

Between the Soviet declaration of war on Japan and the enemy's surrender, the Soviets fought against Japanese troops in Manchuria and Korea during a six-day "victory parade" that resulted in the deaths of thousands of Soviet fighters. Stalin apparently felt compelled to engage his enemy before Japan surrendered too abruptly, giving him a greater role in the dividing of Japanese-held territories. But the war was over officially on September 2, when Allied officials accepted the surrender of Japanese leaders in Tokyo Bay. A new wave of celebration swept across the United States as V-J Day (Victory in Japan) ended the most destructive war in the history of the world.

THE GREAT CONFLICT ENDED

World War II was the greatest conflagration ever and its ripples may still be felt today. Seventy million people fought in the war worldwide and that fighting ended the lives of at least 45 million military personnel and civilians. The war created 1 million U.S. casualties, approximately 40 percent of which were deaths. (Although the war was largely fought a great distance from U.S. soil, a handful of Japanese firebomb balloons had reached Oregon, where a half dozen civilians had been killed.) It was also the most expensive war ever, with direct military costs totaling $1 trillion, plus property damage of twice that figure.

Yet the United States, alongside its allies, emerged, not only victorious, but in a position of greater power than it had ever known before. U.S. influence and prestige would soar following the conflict. The nation's leaders, especially Roosevelt, would be remembered for their courage and tenacity during the fight. The war also produced a string of U.S. military heroes, including Dwight Eisenhower, Douglas MacArthur, George Marshall, George S. Patton, and Admiral Chester Nimitz. U.S. industrial capacity was yet another hero of the war. Every Allied nation had come to rely on the vast capacity of U.S. factories, mills, and mines to produce all the materiel needed to fight the war. U.S. technology, backed by its industrial infrastructure and a workforce of countless thousands of men and women, had produced more weapons, vehicles, and ordinance than any other industrial power on earth had ever done.

The end of the war also marked a victory for democracy. The 1920s and 1930s had witnessed the rise of the great dictators, and they had been discredited, defeated, and destroyed. Hitler and Mussolini did not survive the war, and various Japanese warlords, including General Tojo, would be tried for war crimes and executed.

The American people, along with the peoples of Allied nations around the world, had sacrificed, and their sufferings were repaid with victory. Yet, even in those final months of the war, as Japan, Germany, Italy, and their allies were facing destruction, a new menace was on the rise. The great alliance of the United States, Britain, and the Soviet Union was already collapsing, as Stalin began taking overt steps to establish Communist governments throughout Eastern Europe. World War II had brought together an unlikely trio of allies. The postwar period would deliver a new conflict in its wake—an ideological struggle that would come to be known as the Cold War.

Chronology

1931–32 Japan seizes Manchuria, a region of northeast Asia divided between Russia and China

1933 Hitler is appointed German chancellor. Five weeks later, Franklin Roosevelt is inaugurated as president of the United States

1935 Italy invades and defeats Ethiopia. U.S. Congress passes the first Neutrality Act

TIMELINE

March 13, 1938
Hitler annexes Austria

1931–32
Japan seizes Manchuria

1933
Hitler is appointed German chancellor. Franklin Roosevelt is inaugurated as president of the United States

July 7, 1937
Japanese and Chinese troops fight starting full-scale war between the two Asian powers

| 1931 | 1932 | 1933 | 1934 | 1935 | 1936 | 1937 | 1938 |

1935
Italy invades and defeats Ethiopia. U.S. Congress passes the first Neutrality Act

1936
The Spanish Civil War opens

Nov 3, 1938
Japanese proclaim a "new order in Asia"

1936 The Spanish Civil War opens. Hitler and Italian leader Mussolini form the Rome–Berlin Axis. Second Neutrality Act is passed. FDR is reelected to a second term as president

1937

July 7 Japanese and Chinese troops fight one another at the Marco Polo Bridge near Peking (today's Beijing), ushering in full-scale war between the two Asian powers

1938

March 13 Hitler annexes Austria (the *Anschluss*), then demands the liberation of German people living in the Sudetenland region of Czechoslovakia

Sept 3, 1939 Britain and France declare war on Germany	**Dec 7, 1941** The Japanese attack the US Pacific Fleet at Pearl Harbor, Hawaii	**May 13, 1943** British and U.S. forces defeat the Axis forces in North Africa	**Sept 2, 1945** Japan's surrender
	Dec 8, 1941 Britain and the United States declare war on Japan	**Aug 17, 1943** The Allies take Sicily	**Aug 6, 1945** U.S. Air Force drops an atomic bomb on Hiroshima
			May 8, 1945 Victory in Europe (V-E Day) is celebrated

1939 1940 1941 1942 1943 1944 1945 1946

May 24–June 10, 1940 The Dunkirk Evacuation	**June 22, 1941** Hitler initiates Operation Barbarossa against Russia	**Jan 1944** The siege of Leningrad is ended by the Soviet army	**April 30, 1945** Hitler commits suicide
June 22, 1940 France signs an armistice with Germany, taking France into German occupation	**June 4, 1942** The United States defeats the Japanese navy at the Battle of Midway	**June 6, 1944** D-Day	**Feb 19, 1945** U.S. Marines land on Iwo Jima
		Dec 16, 1944 The Battle of the Bulge begins	

September 29 The Munich Accords: Hitler, Chamberlain, Daladier, and Mussolini meet in Munich and agree that Hitler should have the Sudetenland in Czechoslovakia. Chamberlain returns to England with a piece of paper signed by Hitler, proclaiming "peace in our time"

November 3 Japanese proclaim a "new order in Asia," declaring their intention to dominate Asia

1939

March Hitler invades Czechoslovakia

August Russia and Germany sign a non-aggression pact that includes secret clauses for the division of Poland

September 1 Hitler invades Poland

September 3 Britain and France declare war on Germany

September–May (1940) The months following Britain's declaration of war are referred to as the "phony war" because Britain sees no military action

November 4 New U.S. Neutrality Act enables the sale of arms to the Allies on a cash-and-carry basis only

1940

April–May Hitler invades Denmark and Norway

May 10 Hitler launches his *Blitzkrieg* (lightning war) against the Netherlands and Belgium. Both countries are occupied

May 13 Winston Churchill becomes the new British prime minister

May 24–June 10 The Dunkirk Evacuation: British and French troops are transported off the beaches of Dunkirk in northern France and brought back to Britain

June 10 Italy enters the war on side of Axis powers, declaring war on Britain and France

June 22 France signs an armistice with Germany, taking France out of the war and into German occupation

July 10–October 31 The Battle of Britain: The RAF defends the skies over Britain and by October 31 the raids have ceased

Sept 27 The Tripartite Pact: This pact of mutual alliance is signed by Germany, Italy, and Japan

September 26 Roosevelt announces an embargo on strategic exports to Japan

October 28 Italy invades Greece

November FDR is elected to a third term as president

December The British rout Italian forces in North Africa

1941

Early 1941 Italy and Germany attack Yugoslavia, Greece, and the island of Crete. German Field Marshall Erwin Rommel leads the Axis powers back to North Africa

June 22 Hitler initiates Operation Barbarossa, sending 3 million soldiers and 3,500 tanks into Russia. Stalin immediately signs a mutual assistance treaty with Britain and launches an eastern front battle that will claim 20 million casualties. The United States, which has been supplying arms to Britain under a "Lend-Lease" agreement, offers similar aid to the U.S.S.R.

August 14 Roosevelt and Churchill publish the Atlantic Charter

September 8 The Germans lay siege to Leningrad

December 7 The Japanese attack the US Pacific Fleet at Pearl Harbor, Hawaii, as a preliminary to taking British, French, and Dutch colonies in Southeast Asia

December 8 Britain and the United States declare war on Japan

December 10 Guam surrenders, becoming the first U.S. possession to fall to the Japanese

December 25 Hong Kong falls to Japan

1942

February 15 The Japanese capture Singapore from the British, taking some 60,000 prisoners

February 19 FDR issues Executive Order 9066, ordering the internment of Japanese-Americans

May 7–8 Battle of the Coral Sea

June 4 The United States defeats the Japanese navy at the Battle of Midway

August The German siege against Stalingrad opens

August 12–13 Stalin meets with Churchill in Moscow to discuss the establishment of a second major front in France

October 23 The Battle of El Alamein in Egypt: British Field Marshal Montgomery attacks the German-Italian army in North Africa, driving the enemy back by 1,500 miles (2,400 km)

November 8 British and U.S. forces under the command of General Dwight Eisenhower land in Northwest Africa, taking control of French Morocco and Algeria

November 12 Naval phase of the Guadalcanal campaign commences

1943

January 24 The Casablanca Conference between Churchill and Roosevelt determines the Allies will fight until the unconditional surrender of the Axis powers

February 1 Japanese forces evacuate Guadalcanal

February 2 Germans surrender to Soviets in Stalingrad

May 13 British and U.S. forces defeat the Axis forces in North Africa

July 10 The Allies invade Sicily

August 17 The Allies take Sicily

September 8 Mussolini is thrown out of office and the new government of Italy surrenders to Britain and the United States. The Germans take control of the

Italian army, free Mussolini from imprisonment and set him up as head of a puppet government in Northern Italy, blocking any further Allied advance through Italy

November Stalin, Roosevelt, and Churchill meet in Tehran to coordinate plans for a simultaneous squeeze on Germany. FDR promises Stalin the establishment of a western front in Europe within the following six months

1944

January The siege of Leningrad is ended by the Soviet army

June 4 Rome is liberated by the Allies

June 6 D-Day: The Allies launch an attack on Germany's forces in Normandy, Western France

June 19–20 The U.S. Navy defeats the Japanese at the battle of the Philippine Sea

July British forces push the Japanese from Burma

July 9 Saipan falls to the Americans

July 21 U.S. Marines assault Guam, Mariana Islands

August 25 The Allies liberate Paris from the Germans

October 20 General MacArthur returns to Philippines

November FDR is elected to a fourth term as president

December 16 The Battle of the Bulge begins: German troops launch a final defensive through the Ardennes region of Belgium. However, they are beaten back by the Allies

1945

February 4 Stalin, FDR, and Churchill meet at Yalta

February 19 U.S. Marines land on Iwo Jima

March 7 Allies cross the Rhine at Remagen, while Soviet forces approach Berlin from the east

April 1 U.S. Marines and soldiers land on Okinawa

April 12 President Roosevelt dies. He is succeeded by President Truman

April 16 Soviet forces begin the Battle of Berlin

April 28 Mussolini is captured and executed by Italian partisans

April 30 Hitler commits suicide in his bombproof shelter

May 2 German forces in Italy surrender to the Allies

May 4 German forces in northwest Germany, Holland, and Denmark surrender to Montgomery

May 7 German Admiral Donitz offers unconditional surrender

May 8 Victory in Europe (V-E Day) is celebrated

June 22 Okinawa falls to the 10th U.S. Army

July 5 Churchill loses election to Clement Atlee's Labour Party

July 17–August 2 Truman, Stalin, and Churchill (later, Clement Attlee) meet at the Potsdam Conference in Potsdam, Germany

August 6 U.S. Air Force drops an atomic bomb on Hiroshima. The Japanese generals refuse to surrender.

August 8 Soviet Union declares war on Japan and invades Japanese-ruled Manchuria

August 9 A second atomic bomb is dropped, on Nagasaki, Japan

August 14 The Japanese unconditionally surrender to the Allies

September 2 U.S. General Douglas MacArthur accepts Japan's surrender, formally ending World War II

Glossary

Allies Refers to the nations who opposed the Axis during World War II. They were led by the "Big Three"—the United States, Britain, and the Soviet Union—and included such minor powers as Australia, Belgium, Canada, China, Free France, Holland, Mexico, India, New Zealand, Norway, Poland, Brazil, Greece, and South Africa.

armistice An agreement by all sides engaged in war to stop fighting.

Axis and **Axis Powers** Included the nations opposed to the Allies during World War II. The three major Axis powers were Germany, Italy, and Japan, and minor powers included Hungary, Rumania, Bulgaria, and Yugoslavia.

Barbarossa (Operation Barbarossa) The German invasion of Russia that began in June 1941.

Bataan A peninsula in the Philippines, site of the retreat of U.S. Army troops in the Philippines in 1942.

Battle of Britain The German air attack on Britain during the summer and fall of 1940.

Battle of the Bulge A failed Nazi counter-offensive launched late in the war, from December 1944 to January 1945.

Battle of Midway A major naval battle in which the U.S. Navy defeated a Japanese attack on Midway Island in the Pacific Ocean during June 4–7, 1942.

Casablanca Conference A summit held between the United States and Britain, at which FDR and Churchill agreed that Germany must surrender unconditionally.

Cold War The continual, but low-level tension that existed between the West, led by the United States, and the Soviet Union from the end of World War II until 1991.

Coral Sea A sea located northeast of Australia. It was the site of a major naval battle in May 1942.

D-Day June 6, 1944—the day that the Allied invasion of occupied Europe began with the landing of troops on the beaches of Normandy in northern France.

Dresden A city in northern Germany, target of Allied fire-bombing during February 13–14, 1945.

El Alamein Location in Egypt of a British offensive that began in October 1942.

Enola Gay Name of the U.S. B-29 bomber that dropped the first atomic bomb (code-named "Little Boy") over Hiroshima, Japan, on August 6, 1945.

fascism A political philosophy that emphasizes the power of the state as it reduces the importance of the individual. It often exalts a race or ethnic group.

Guadalcanal An island in the Solomon Island group in the Pacific, taken from the Japanese by the Allies in 1942.

Guam Largest of the Mariana Islands in the Pacific Ocean. Guam was invaded by the Japanese in 1941, and recaptured by the United States in 1944.

Hiroshima The Japanese city targeted by the United States as the site for the dropping of the first atomic bomb to be used in wartime, on August 6, 1945.

hyperinflation An economic circumstance that occurs when the inflation rate skyrockets, often resulting in the destruction of a country's economy.

interventionist One who believes in the role of a state to participate in foreign events and affairs, including military action.

Iwo Jima A Pacific island taken by the Allies in February–March 1945.

League of Nations An international representative body established during the Versailles Conference to encourage peace and cooperative efforts between nations.

Lend-Lease Act A law passed by Congress on March 11, 1941, that gave President Roosevelt the authority to sell, transfer, or ease war goods to any Allied nation.

Leyte Island (Leyte Gulf) An island in the Philippines, retaken by the Allies in an amphibious assault on October 20, 1944.

Luftwaffe The German air force.

magic U.S. code word for intercepted and decrypted Japanese diplomatic codes and ciphers.

Manhattan Project A secret U.S. Army project, initiated in 1942, with the aim of developing an atomic bomb before Germany or the Soviet Union did so.

Munich Accords An agreement signed by Germany, Britain, France, and Italy in September 1938, which gave Germany permission to annex the Sudetenland region of Czechoslovakia.

Nazi Party The National Socialist German Workers' Party, founded by Adolf Hitler in 1921.

New Deal President Franklin Roosevelt's economic programs and strategies implemented during the 1930s to battle the economic depression in the United States.

Normandy The area of northern France invaded by the Allies on D-Day.

Okinawa A Pacific island in the Ryukyu group, south of Japan.

Omaha Beach One of the Normandy beaches in northern France where U.S. forces landed on D-Day.

Overlord (Operation Overlord) The code name for the Allied invasion of occupied Europe that began on D-Day, June 6, 1944.

Panzer A German tank or tank unit.

partisan Refers to paramilitary forces who operated behind the front lines during World War II.

Pearl Harbor The U.S. naval base on Hawaii is attacked by the Japanese on December 7, 1941, bringing the United States into World War II.

Potsdam Conference A summit between the United States, Britain, and the Soviet Union that opened mid-July, 1945, and was held in the German town of Potsdam.

Rome–Berlin Alliance A signed agreement between Hitler and Mussolini in 1936 that created the Axis.

Royal Air Force (RAF) The British air force.

Ryukyus A Pacific island group south of Japan.

Saipan One of the Marianas Islands in the western Pacific Ocean.

Sealion (Operation Sealion) Code name for the planned German air invasion of Britain in late 1940.

Solomon Islands A 600-mile (1,000-km) long chain of islands in the Pacific.

Teheran Conference A summit between the United States, Britain, and the Soviet Union held between November 8 and December 1, 1943. Roosevelt, Churchill, and Stalin met for the first time at this conference.

Torch (Operation Torch) Code name for the Allied invasion of North Africa that began in November 1942.

Trinity Code name for the site where the first atomic bomb was tested in New Mexico in 1945.

V-E Day May 8, 1945, Victory in Europe Day—when Germany surrendered in World War II.

V-J Day August 15, 1945, Victory in Japan Day—when Japan surrendered in World War II.

Versailles Conference The international forum following World War I, led by the United States, France, Britain, and Italy, that drew up a peace treaty.

Wehrmacht The German military.

Bibliography

Abrams, Richard. *Sixty Years of Revolutionary Change: 1940–2000.* New York: Cambridge University Press, 2006.

Ambrose, Stephen. *American Heritage New History of World War II.* New York: Viking, 1997.

————. *The Victors: Eisenhower and His Boys: The Men of World War II.* New York: Simon & Schuster, 1998.

Axelrod, Alan. *The Real History of World War II: A New Look at the Past.* New York: Sterling Publishing Company, 2008.

Davis, David A. *Lightning Strike: The Secret Mission to Kill Admiral Yamamoto and Avenge Pearl Harbor.* New York: St. Martin's Press, 2006.

Editors of Time-Life Books. *This Fabulous Century: 1930–1940.* New York: Time-Life Books, 1969.

Elson, Robert T. *Prelude to War.* Alexandria, VA: Time-Life Books, 1977.

Hixson, Walter. *Pearl Harbor in History and Memory: The American Experience in World War II, Volume IV.* Philadelphia: Francis and Taylor, Inc., 2002.

Kennedy, David M. *Freedom From Fear: The American People in Depression and War, 1929–1945.* New York: Oxford University Press, 1999.

Leuchtenburg, William E. *The Supreme Court Reborn: The Constitutional Revolution in Age of Roosevelt.* New York: Oxford University Press, 1995.

Miller, Nathan. *War at Sea: A Naval History of World War II.* Oxford University Press, 1997.

Porch, Douglas. *The Path to Victory: The Mediterranean Theater in World War II.* New York: Farrar, Straus, and Giroux, 2004.

Remini, Robert V. *A Short History of the United States.* New York: HarperCollins, 2008.

Bibliography

Tierney, Dominic. *FDR and the Spanish Civil War: Neutrality and Commitment in the Struggle that Divided America.* Durham, NC: Duke University Press, 2007.

Tindall, George and David Shi. *America: A Narrative History.* New York: W. W. Norton & Company, 1997.

Toland, John. *Adolf Hitler.* Garden City, NY: Doubleday & Company, Inc., 1976.

————. *Infamy: Pearl Harbor and Its Aftermath.* Garden City, NY: Doubleday, 1982.

Weinstein, Allen. *The Story of America: Freedom and Crisis From Settlement to Superpower.* New York: DK Books, 2002.

Further Resources

Ambrose, Stephen. *Good Fight: How World War II Was Won.* New York: Simon & Schuster Adult Publishing Group, 2001.

Barr, Gary E. *World War II Home Front.* Portsmouth, NH: Heinemann Library, 2004.

Barry, Rick. *Gunner's Run: A World War II Novel.* Greenville, SC: JourneyForth Books, 2007.

Boyne, John. *The Boy in the Striped Pyjamas.* New York: Random House Children's Books, 2007.

Bruchac, Joseph. *Code Talker: A Novel About the Navajo Marines of World War Two.* New York: Penguin Group (USA), 2006.

Connolly, Sean. *World War II.* Portsmouth, NH: Heinemann Library, 2003.

Darman, Peter. *World War II: A Day-by-Day History.* New York: Barnes and Noble, 2007.

Gerdes, Louise. *World War II.* Farmington Hills, MI: Cengage Gale, 2004.

Holiday, Laurel. *Children in the Holocaust and World War II: Their Secret Diaries.* New York: Simon & Schuster Adult Publishing Group, 1996.

Houston, James A. *Farewell to Manzanar: A True Sory of Japanese American Experience During and After the World War II Internment.* New York: Houghton Mifflin Harcourt, 2002.

McNeese, Tim. *Battle of the Bulge.* Philadelphia: Chelsea House Publishers, 2004.

————. *Stalingrad.* Philadelphia: Chelsea House Publishers, 2003.

Messenger, Charles. *World War II.* New York: DK Publishing, Inc., 2004.

Further Resources

Panchyk, Richard. *World War II for Kids: A History With 21 Activities*. Chicago: Chicago Review Press, Inc., 2002.

Senker, Carl. *World War II*. Farmington Hills, MI: Cengage Gale, 2005.

Web sites

British armed forces:
  http://www.fleetairarm.com/
  http://www.rafmuseum.org.uk/
  http://www.iwm.org.uk/

Concentration Camps and the Holocaust:
  http://en.auschwitz.org.pl/m/
  http://www.ushmm.org/

Museums with exhibits related to WWII:
  http://www.atomicmuseum.com
  http://www.navalaviationmuseum.org
  http://www.nationalww2museum.org
  http://www.history.army.mil/

U.S. Armed Forces:
  http://www.tecom.usmc.mil/mcu/mcrcweb/index.htm
  http://www.usmcmuseum.com/
  http://www.airpowermuseum.org/
  http://www.nasm.si.edu/museum/udvarhazy/

War in the Pacific:
  http://www.pcf.city.hiroshima.jp/
  http://www.nps.gov/valr/index.htm
  http://www.pearlharborattacked.com/

Picture Credits

Page

10: The Granger Collection, NYC/TopFoto

22: Â © Ullsteinbild/TopFoto TopFoto.co.uk

32: Â © Ullsteinbild/TopFoto TopFoto.co.uk

46: Topham Picturepoint Topfoto.co.uk

57: The Granger Collection, NYC/TopFoto

59: Illustration by Gerald Wood

61: The Granger Collection, NYC/TopFoto

67: The Granger Collection, NYC/TopFoto

73: RIA Novosti/TopFoto TopFoto.co.uk

77: Illustration by John James

89: The Granger Collection, NYC/TopFoto

92: Library of Congress

100: The Granger Collection, NYC/TopFoto

104: Illustration by John James

108: Topham/AP TopFoto.co.uk

113: Topham/AP TopFoto.co.uk

136: Courtesy of Abbott Studio, www.abbottsudio.com

Index

A

"ABC-1 Agreement," 69
Abraham Lincoln Brigade, 29
Africa, 74–79
air raids, 76–77, 106–107
Antares, USS, 9
anti-Semitism, 21, 103
Arizona, USS, 10, 60
Atlantic Charter, 71
atomic bomb, 110–111, 112, 113
Austria, annexation of, 36

B

Bataan Death March, 66
Battle of Britain (1940), 46–47
blacks, opportunities for, 90–91
Blitzkrieg (lightning war), 36, 42
Bloch, Rear Admiral C. C., 11
bombing raids, 76–77, 106–107
Braceros, 88–90
Bradley, General Omar, 101, 102–103,
    105
Bulge, Battle of the (1944-45), 101–102
Burma, 65

C

Cairo Declaration (1943), 80–81
California, USS, 60
casualties of the war, 83
Chamberlain, Neville, 36–37, 38, 44
Chiang Kai-shek, 53
China, 25, 29, 31, 32, 33–36, 53, 81
Churchill, Winston, 37, 44, 48, 69–71,
    74–79, 78–79, 80, 104–105, 112
"code talkers," 93–94
concentration camps, 103
Condor, USS, 9

conserving resources, 84–85
Coral Sea, Battle of the (1942), 66
Crow, Joseph Medicine, 93
Cuba, 17
Czechoslovakia, 36, 37

D

D-Day Landings, 72, 97–100
Dawes Plan, 19
Declaration of Cairo (1943), 80–81
Denmark, 42
Depression, the, 15–18
Dunkirk, evacuation of, 44

E

Earle, Captain John B., 11
economy, 83–87
Einstein, Albert, 110
Eisenhower, General Dwight D., 72, 78,
    98–99, 105, 115
El Alamein, Battle of (1942), 75, 78

F

Fall Gelb (Operation Yellow), 42
Fall Weiss (Operation White),
    39–40
"Final Solution," the, 103
Finland, 41
Five-Power Naval Treaty (1922), 27
France, 28, 36–37, 43–45, 101
Franco, General Francisco, 28–29,
    36
Fuchida, Commander Mitsuo, 8, 11

G

Germany, 19–22, 28, 36–40, 42–47, 52,
    56, 69–71, 72–80, 97–106

Great Britain, 36–37, 38–40, 44, 46–47, 55, 69–71, 75–81, 99
Greer, USS, 50
Grew, Joseph, 51
gross national product (GNP), 84
Guadalcanal, 68–69
Guam, 65

H
Havana Conference (1940), 49
Hess, Rudolf, 22
Hindenburg, Paul von, 20
Hiroshima, 112, 113
Hitler, Adolf, 19–22, 28–29, 36–37, 39–40, 44, 45, 72, 74, 80, 102, 103, 105–106
Hitler–Stalin Pact (1939), 39
Hull, Cordell, 17, 32, 52, 55

I
Indianapolis, USS, 17–18
industry, 86–87
internment camps, 12, 94–95
Italy, 28, 45, 52, 80–81
Italian internment, 12
Iwo Jima (1944), 107–109

J
Japan, 23–25, 51–63, 66–69, 106–114
    invasion of China, 27, 29, 31, 32, 33–36
    Pearl Harbor (1941), 7–11, 54–55, x56–63
Japanese in the U.S. military, 95–96
Japanese internment, 12, 94–95
Jiang Jeishi, 53

K
kamikaze pilots, 109
Kearny, USS, 50
Konoye, Prince Fumimaro, 51, 55
Korea, 81, 115

L
League of Nations, 21, 25, 26, 28
Lend-Lease Act (1941), 42–43, 49
Leningrad, siege of, 72–73
Leyte Gulf, Battle of (1944), 107
London Economic Conference (1933), 16–18, 26
Lubbe, Marinus van der, 20

M
MacArthur, Chief of Staff Douglas, 26, 66, 106, 115
Maignot Line, 43, 44–45
Malaya, 65
Manhattan Project, 110–111
Marshall, General George C., 72, 115
Maryland, USS, 60
Matsuoka, Yosuke, 52
Mexican workers, 88–90
Mexico, 17
Midway, Battle of (1942), 67–68
military areas, US, 12
Montgomery, General Bernard, 75, 78, 79, 102, 103
Moscow, siege of, 72–73
Munich Accords, 37
Mussolini, Benito, 18, 28–29, 36, 45, 80

N
Nagasaki, 112
national debt, 85
National Association for the Advancement of Colored People (NAACP), 91
National Defense Act (1940), 45–46
National Socialist German Workers Party (Nazis), 19–21
Native Americans, during the war, 91–94
neutrality acts, 30–32, 40–41, 50
Nevada, USS, 60
New Deal, the, 15–18, 83
New Guinea, 66
New York World's Fair, 34–35

Nimitz, Admiral Chester "Chesty," 66, 68, 115

Normandy invasion *See* D-Day Landings

North Africa, 74–79

Norway, 42

O

Office of Price Administration (OPA), 87

oil embargo, Japanese, 55

Okinawa (1944), 109

Oklahoma, USS, 62

Operation Magic, 52

Operation Market Garden, 102

Operation Overlord *See* D-Day Landings

Operation Torch, 78

Operation White (*Fall Weiss*), 39–40

Operation Yellow (*Fall Gelb*), 42

Oppenheimer, J. Robert, 111

Outerbridge, Lieutenant William, 9

P

Patton, General George S., 79, 101, 115

Pearl Harbor (1941), 7–11, 54–55, 56–63

Philippines, the, 53, 54, 65, 66, 107

"Phony War," 41

Poland, 38–40

Potsdam Conference (1945), 112

prisoners of war, 12

Q

"Quarantine Speech," 33

R

Ramsey, Lieutenant Commander Logan, 60

"Rape of Nanking," 34–36

rationing, 84–85

Reuben James, USS, 50

Rommel, Field Marshall Erwin, 75, 78, 99, 100

Roosevelt, Franklin Delano, 26, 37, 52, 74, 78–79, 80, 86, 94, 101, 110

  "ABC-1 Agreement," 69

  Atlantic Charter, 71

  attack on Pearl Harbor (1941), 58–59

  death of, 105

  "Good Neighbor" policy, 16–17

  Japanese oil embargo, 55

  Lend-Lease Act (1941), 42–43, 49

  National Defense Act (1940), 45–46

  neutrality acts, 30–32, 40–41, 50

  New Deal, 15–18, 83

  "Quarantine Speech," 33

  re-elected, 47–49

  Spanish Civil War (1936-39), 29

  support for China, 53

S

Sicily, 79

Singapore, 65

Sino-Japanese War (1937-45), 25, 29, 31, 32, 33–36, 53

Skorzeny, Otto, 80

Smith–Connally Anti-Strike Act (1943), 87

Soviet Union, 16, 18, 39, 41, 56, 72–74, 102, 104–105

Spanish Civil War (1936-39), 28–29

Stalin, Josef, 18, 38, 39, 40, 74, 80, 112

Stimson, Henry, 86–87

T

Taft, Robert, 43

taxation, 85

Tennessee, USS, 10, 60, 61

Third Reich, the, 21

Tojo, Lieutenant General Hideki, 52, 55

Tripartite Act (1940), 52, 53

Truman, Harry, 96, 112

U
unions, 87
United Nations, 71

V
V-E Day (Victory in Europe), 106
V-J Day (Victory in Japan), 114
Versailles Treaty (1919), 19, 21, 23

W
War Production Board (WPB), 86
War Relocation Camps, 12, 94–95
Ward, USS, 9–10, 56

Washington Naval Treaty (1922), 24
West Virginia, USS, 10, 61
Whalen, Grover, 34
Willkie, Wendell, 48–49
Wilson, Woodrow, 25
women in WWII, 87–88
World's Fair, New York, 34–35

Y
Yamamoto, Admiral Isoroku, 54, 56
Yamashita, General Tomoyuki, 53
Yorktown, USS, 67

About the Author

Tim McNeese is associate professor of history at York College in York, Nebraska. Professor McNeese holds degrees from York College, Harding University, and Missouri State University. He has published more than 100 books and educational materials. His writing has earned him a citation in the library reference work, *Contemporary Authors* and multiple citations in *Best Books for Young Teen Readers*. In 2006, Tim appeared on the History Channel program, *Risk Takers, History Makers: John Wesley Powell and the Grand Canyon*. He was been a faculty member at the Tony Hillerman Writers Conference in Albuquerque. His wife, Beverly, is assistant professor of English at York College. They have two married children, Noah and Summer, and five grandchildren—Ethan, Adrianna, Finn William, Ari, and Beckett Percy. Tim and Bev have sponsored college study trips on the Lewis and Clark Trail, to the American Southwest, and to New England. You may contact Professor McNeese at tdmcneese@york.edu.

About the Consultant

Richard Jensen is Research Professor at Montana State University, Billings. He has published 11 books on a wide range of topics in American political, social, military, and economic history, as well as computer methods. After taking a Ph.D. at Yale in 1966, he taught at numerous universities, including Washington, Michigan, Harvard, Illinois-Chicago, West Point, and Moscow State University in Russia.